SALVATION

MARK R. JACKSON

Wasteland Press

Shelbyville, KY USA
www.wastelandpress.net

Salvation
by Mark R. Jackson

First Printing – December 2018
ISBN: 978-1-68111-275-6
Library of Congress Control Number: 2018965329

Printed in the U.S.A.

0   1   2   3   4   5   6   7   8

This book is dedicated to my children, Graham and Savannah, with the prayer that they will grow up to experience, cherish, and tell others about the salvation described in this book.

TABLE OF CONTENTS

INTRODUCTION

༄༅།

Have you ever rescued someone from a life-threatening situation? Maybe you're a fireman or a nurse, and you stepped in at just the right time to save someone's life. You carried them out of a burning building or you did CPR on them. They would have died, but you rescued them. You saved their life. On the other hand, maybe you were the one who was rescued. You were drowning in a lake or choking on a piece of food. Then someone dove in and brought you safely to shore, or they did the Heimlich to remove the foreign object so you could breathe again. Whether you have rescued someone or been rescued yourself (or have seen situations like these), you already know something about salvation.

Salvation is a word or concept that is not too difficult to understand. It simply means deliverance. To be saved is to be delivered or rescued from a perilous situation. Of course, the examples above speak of human acts of salvation. What we will be looking at in this book is the divine act of salvation. God saves us not simply from drowning or choking, but from the consequences and control of sin. The Bible does at times speak of God's salvation in terms of deliverance from physical harm or oppression, acts of divine healing, and even military triumph, especially in the Old Testament. But the focus of this book will be on what we may call spiritual salvation—salvation from sin. This is the primary focus of salvation in the New Testament, and salvation from sin is present in the Old Testament as well (Ps 39.8; 79.9; 130.8; Isa 59.1-2; Ezek

1

3.18). This type of salvation can be defined as follows: "The divine act of delivering a believer from the power and curse of sin and then restoring that individual to the fellowship with God for which humans were originally intended."[1] This salvation certainly has physical and social ramifications, but the emphasis is on being divinely rescued from sin itself.

Salvation is a key, pervasive theme in Scripture. In many ways, it is the main theme or message.[2] Even in terms of God, Christopher Wright points out, "The God revealed as Yahweh in the Old Testament, and in Jesus of Nazareth in the New Testament, is above all else the God who saves. That is the distinctive mark of his uniqueness and the defining mark of his identity."[3] That is why John Stott writes, "The Bible is essentially a handbook of salvation."[4] We see this in the story line of Scripture. The Bible begins on a glorious note. The first verse states, "In the beginning, God created the heavens and the earth" (Gen 1.1). With divine intent, God created this world out of nothing, and he created it in a state of goodness. Six times in the first chapter of Genesis it says that God saw what he had made and it was "good" (vv. 4, 10, 12, 18, 21, 25), and after creating his crowning jewel—humanity made in his image, it says that God saw that it was "very good" (v. 31). Everything was wonderful. The only problem at this point was that Adam had no human

---

[1] Millard J. Erickson, *The Concise Dictionary of Christian Theology*, Rev. ed. (Wheaton, IL: Crossway Books, 2001), 175. The main verb used in the Old Testament is *yasa'* ("to save, deliver, help, set free"). Along with its derivatives, it is used over 350 times. In the New Testament, the main verb is *sōzō* ("to save, rescue, deliver, heal"), which is used 106 times. The main noun is *sōtēria* ("salvation, deliverance"). It occurs 45 times.

[2] Bruce Demarest, *The Cross and Salvation* (Wheaton, IL: Crossway Books, 1997), 25.

[3] Christopher J. H. Wright, *Salvation Belongs to Our God* (Downers Grove, IL: IVP Academic, 2007), 51.

[4] John Stott, *The Message of 2 Timothy* (Downers Grove, IL: Inter-Varsity, 1973), 102.

companion, but God soon solved this dilemma by creating a wife for him (Gen 2.18-25). Thus, there was harmony, bliss, and God's good creation. But things were about to change.

God had one rule at this point which he gave to Adam. "The LORD God commanded the man, saying, 'You may surely eat of every tree of the garden, but of the tree of the knowledge of good and evil you shall not eat, for in the day that you eat of it you will surely die'" (Gen 2.16-17). Adam and Eve could enjoy every tree in the garden, just not this tree. So, the emphasis was on all that they could do, but they focused on the one thing they couldn't do. That's how Satan attacks us still today. God has given us so much freedom and blessings, but we desire what is forbidden. Therefore, Adam and Eve, at the instigation of Satan, ate from the forbidden tree and were banished from the Garden of Eden (Gen 3.1-24). Sin entered the world and death too as a consequence of sin.[5] Actually, everything bad in the world can be traced back to this one horrible decision.

God's response to this act of rebellion was to eject them from the garden, but that was not his only response. He also made a promise to them that one of their descendants would crush the head of their enemy, the devil (Gen 3.15). Scripture makes it clear that the serpent in the garden was Satan, also known as the devil (Rom 16.20; Rev 12.9; 20.2). This promise in Genesis 3 is known as the *protoevangelium* ("the first gospel"). This is the first promise of good news recorded in the Bible. Humanity fell into sin, but God's rescue mission was underway with a promise.

The rest of the Bible traces how this promise of salvation, which included the defeat of Satan, came to fruition in Jesus Christ. God said, "He will crush your head, and you will strike his heel" (Gen 3.15 NIV). Notice the difference between the head and the heel. The seed of woman would administer to Satan a death blow to the head, whereas Satan would strike the heel of the promised seed. The seed would suffer and be

---

[5] God said, "...in the day that you eat of it you will surely die" (Gen 2.17). Adam and Eve did not physically die on that day, but they did die spiritually. On that day they were separated from intimate fellowship with God and banned from the tree of life in the garden.

hurt, but he would recover. The devil, on the other hand, would be destroyed. This seed refers to Jesus Christ, the promised redeemer of fallen humanity (Gal 3.16). This seed can be traced through the Old Testament. He would come through the line of...

- *Abraham* (Gen 12.1-3)

- *Isaac*, not Ishmael (Gen 26.2-4)

- *Jacob*, not Esau (Gen 28.10-14)

- *Judah*, not his brothers (Gen 49.10)

- *David*, not his brothers or Saul (1 Sam 16.1-13)

- *Solomon*, not his brothers (2 Sam 7.8-16; 1 Kings 1.28-40)

This seed can be traced through these Old Testament characters culminating with Jesus of Nazareth, who was that promised seed or offspring (Matt 1.1-17). Thus, the redeemer would come from the seed of woman. This shows that he would be fully human. Yet, this redeemer would also defeat Satan and so he would have to be divine. That is what Jesus Christ is, both fully God and fully man.

Jesus is the fulfillment of the promise made in Genesis 3.15. More than that, he is the fulfillment of *all* the promises made in the Old Testament about God's plan to save humanity. Second Corinthians 1.20 says, "All the promises of God find their Yes in him." God's plan to save us finds its fulfillment in Jesus. Actually, the name Jesus means "Yahweh saves." That's why the angel said to Joseph, "She will bear a son, and you shall call his name Jesus, for he will save his people from their sins" (Matt 1.21). He was called Jesus because his mission was salvation. More than a teacher or a prophet or a healer, Jesus was a Savior. In fact, he was *the* Savior.[6] As it says in

---

[6] Of course, God the Father is Savior too. He planned salvation, while Jesus purchased it by his death and resurrection. Wright points out that in the New Testament the title "Savior" (*sōtēr*) is reserved for God and Jesus alone. Eight times God is called Savior, and sixteen times Jesus is (*Salvation Belongs to Our God*, 43).

Acts 4.12, "There is salvation in no one else, for there is no other name under heaven given among men by which we must be saved." This verse teaches that salvation is essential ("we must be saved"), and it is found in Jesus Christ alone ("no other name"). Only Jesus can save us from sin and death.

The salvation Jesus offers us is comprehensive in nature. Salvation, as described in the New Testament, "became, probably very early, a technical term to sum up all the blessings brought about by the gospel."[7] It involves our deliverance from sin from our initial conversion to our glorification in heaven. This can be seen in that salvation is past, present, and future. We have been saved, we are being saved, and we will be saved. We have been forgiven of all our sins, we are being transformed progressively into the likeness of Christ, and when he returns we will receive a new, sin-immune, immortal, glorified body.

- Past salvation — "For by grace *you have been saved* through faith" (Eph 2.8).

- Present salvation — "For the word of the cross is folly to those who are perishing, but to us *who are being saved* it is the power of God" (1 Cor 1.18).

- Future salvation — "Much more then, being now justified by his blood, *we shall be saved* from wrath through him" (Rom 5.9 KJV).[8]

Such a full and comprehensive salvation deserves our praise. An important motivation of mine in writing this book is to stress that biblical salvation is *God-given* and *God-glorifying*. Salvation comes

---

[7] Michael Green, *The Meaning of Salvation* (Vancouver, BC: Regent College Publishing, 1998), 143.

[8] The italics in these verses were added. For more verses on each of these aspects of salvation, see Rom 8.24; Col 1.13; 2 Tim 1.9; Tit 3.5 (past); Acts 2.47; 1 Cor 15.2; 2 Cor 2.15; Phil 2.12; Heb 7.25; 1 Pet 2.2 (present); Rom 13.11; 1 Cor 3.15; Phil 3.20; 1 Thess 5.8; 2 Tim 4.18; Heb 9.28 (future).

from God and brings him glory. As it says in Isaiah 12.2, "Behold, God is my salvation." Thus, there is no such thing as self-salvation. We do not save ourselves, nor can the church or a sacrament save us. Even faith is not the basis of our salvation, but rather the means. God is the one who saves us, and we receive this salvation by faith. From beginning to end, God is our salvation. That's why we should be filled with heartfelt praise and thanksgiving. It's also why we should never be guilty of spiritual pride, self-righteousness, or judgmentalism. The only thing we have to boast about is how great our God is and how great is the salvation he has provided for us. Hebrews 2.3 speaks of "such a great salvation." Let's learn more about this great salvation.

CHAPTER ONE

God's Eternal Plan

◦❧❦❧◦

I became a follower of Jesus Christ on September 23, 1990, at the age of seventeen. After struggling with drug abuse and being in a rehab center for three months, I was converted. I knew that something powerful had happened in my life. That night before I went to bed I prayed, "Lord, lead me down the straight and narrow" (see Matt 7.13-14). I knew I had a lot of changes to make, but I trusted God to lead me and help me with those changes. And he has. My conversion took place on a Sunday in the fall of 1990. However, there was a lot that preceded my salvation, not only in my life but in eternity. *God's plan to save me preceded my belief in him. It also preceded my birth. In fact, it preceded anyone's birth.*

Before We Were Born

Salvation is the eternal plan of God. The Apostle Paul referred to it as "the eternal purpose...realized in Christ Jesus our Lord" (Eph 3.11). Revelation 14.6 speaks of the "eternal gospel." In the chapter before this verse in Revelation, we read about "the Lamb who was slain from the creation of the world" (Rev 13.8 NIV). Jesus was crucified under Pontius Pilate in the early AD 30s. Yet, in the mind and plan of God, he was crucified before the world was ever created. Salvation through the death of Christ was God's eternal plan.

Jesus is not Plan B. He has always been Plan A. Even before God created the world, he foreordained that his Son would die for our sins as an atoning sacrifice. This shows God's great love. He knew we would sin, but he created us anyway. And before we needed a Savior, he planned to send us one. The Apostle Peter explains, "For you know that it was not with perishable things such as silver or gold that you were redeemed from the empty way of life handed down to you from your ancestors, but with the precious blood of Christ, a lamb without blemish or defect. He was chosen before the creation of the world, but was revealed in these last times for your sake" (1 Pet 1.18-20 NIV). Similarly, Paul states, "For God saved us and called us to live a holy life. He did this, not because we deserved it, but because that was his plan from before the beginning of time—to show us his grace through Christ Jesus" (2 Tim 1.9 NLT). The heavenly kingdom that we will enjoy one day because of Christ was prepared for us before we were born. "Then the king will say to those on his right, 'Come, you who are blessed by my Father, inherit the kingdom prepared for you from the foundation of the world'" (Matt 25.34).

Two watershed moments in the history of salvation were the sending of the Son and the sending of the Spirit. Galatians 4.4-6 states, "But when the fullness of time had come, God sent forth his Son, born of woman, born under the law, to redeem those who were under the law, so that we might receive adoption as sons. And because you are sons, God has sent the Spirit of his Son into our hearts, crying, 'Abba! Father!'" God the Father sent his Son to redeem us and adopt us into his family. He also sent the Spirit of his Son (the Holy Spirit) to assure us of our adoption and to preserve us as children of God. Both of these acts of sending occurred before you or I was born. We did not ask God to send his Son or his Spirit. We certainly didn't deserve it. Again, this highlights that salvation preceded our birth and so glorifies the God of all grace (1 Pet 5.10).

In the Old Testament

The gospel of salvation that the apostles preached was not a novel idea or message. It was promised in the Old Testament. Paul calls it "the gospel of God" (Rom 1.1). The gospel comes from God, that is, "the source and authority behind the message" is God himself.[1] This gospel was "promised beforehand through his prophets in the holy Scriptures" (v. 2). This is one of the reasons the Old Testament is so important and still relevant for us as Christians. We no longer live under the old covenant, but the Old Testament as Scripture is divinely inspired and teaches us about salvation through faith in Jesus Christ (2 Tim 3.15-16). Certain commands from the Old Testament are no longer relevant to us as Christians, for they have been fulfilled and set aside by Christ. This includes such commands as circumcision, dietary restrictions, and Sabbath regulations (Gal 6.15; Col 2.16-17). Yet, the moral commands, particularly those reaffirmed in the New Testament, such as do not murder or lie or commit adultery, are still relevant. They are to guide us as redeemed followers of Christ. When the apostles evangelized the Roman Empire, they therefore preached and taught from the Old Testament. Today we have the luxury of preaching the gospel from both the Old and New Testaments.[2]

Salvation is prefigured in the Old Testament. The *sacrificial system* with all its animal sacrifices showed that the shedding of blood was necessary for reconciliation and forgiveness. It also showed that the shedding of animal blood was insufficient. Hebrews 10.4 states, "For it is impossible for the blood of bulls and goats to take away sins." That's why there were continual sacrifices. Day after day, year after year, priests performed sacrifices on behalf of the people, but they could never deal with sin in an ultimate sense. But the sacrifice of Christ, the sinless Lamb of God, atoned for sin once and for all so that no other sacrifice was needed. Jesus died once, and that was enough. That's why from the cross he declared, "It is finished" (John 19.30). As both priest and victim, Jesus gave his life for ours. We

---

[1] James D. G. Dunn, *Romans 1-8* (Nashville: Thomas Nelson Publishers, 1988), 10.

[2] For a good book on the importance and relevance of the Old Testament, see Tremper Longmann III, *Making Sense of the Old Testament* (Grand Rapids, MI: Baker Academic, 1998).

know that his sacrifice was accepted by God because he raised him from the dead. The Book of Hebrews is an excellent book to read to learn more about the all-sufficient, atoning sacrifice of Jesus.

Heroes in the Old Testament point to Jesus as the Savior. Moses led the people of Israel out of Egyptian bondage. He also interceded for them when they were disobedient and exposed to God's judgment. Jesus is greater than Moses, for he delivers us from the bondage of Satan and sin and effectively and continually intercedes for us at God's right hand (John 8.36; Rom 8.34). The name Joshua comes from the Hebrew word for Jesus. Thus, it too means "Yahweh saves." Joshua led God's people into the promised land. Jesus leads us all the way to heaven itself (John 14.1-6). David was a shepherd and a king. Jesus is the good shepherd, the great shepherd, and the chief shepherd (John 10.11; Heb 13.20; 1 Pet 5.4). Moreover, he is the King of kings (Rev 17.14; 19.16). He rules over all other kings and he is the greatest king barring none. His reign will never end (Luke 1.33).

These heroes—Moses, Joshua, and David, and other ones from the Old Testament—were all imperfect. Some, like David, were guilty of glaring sins, for he engaged in adultery and was responsible for murder. He broke at least three of the Ten Commandments, for his adultery was preceded by covetousness. Moses too was guilty of murder. Others sinned as well. Noah got drunk, Abraham lied, and Jonah ran from his calling. The Bible, with absolute frankness, presents its characters warts and all. But this only highlights and points toward Jesus as the provider of salvation. All the heroes of the Old Testament were flawed men and women, and thus were clearly not the promised seed that would bring redemption (Gen 3.15). That seed was Jesus, who was the fulfillment of the Old Testament.

There are *promises* in the Old Testament that are fulfilled in the salvation Jesus provided. A new covenant is predicted (Jer 31.31). A covenant is a solemn agreement between two parties that establishes a relationship between them. The new covenant was ratified and established by the blood of Jesus Christ (Luke 22.20). The old covenant, which is also known as the Mosaic covenant, was powerless in changing the hearts of God's people. It involved the giving of the law. However, the law could only reveal sin; it couldn't remove it. Like a mirror, the law reveals our imperfection and need, but it can't fix our problem. Jesus, on the other hand, died to bring us into a new covenant with God where all our sins are forgiven and our hearts are changed by the presence of his Spirit in our lives. With his Spirit in us, God's law is no longer simply written on tablets of stone; instead, it is written on our hearts, which means we are now willing and able to obey God (Jer 31.33; Ezek 36.26-27). That is why Augustine famously prayed, "Grant what you command, and command what you will" (*Confessions*, 10.29). Only as God grants us the power through his Spirit to obey his commands can we actually do it, and even then we will never do it perfectly in this life.

Speaking of the Spirit, this was another promise of the Old Testament. "And it shall come to pass afterward, that I will pour out my Spirit on all flesh; your sons and your daughters shall prophesy, your old men shall dream dreams, and your young men shall see visions. Even on the male and female servants in those days I will pour out my Spirit" (Joel 2.28-29). Paul refers to the Holy Spirit as "the promised Spirit" (Gal 3.14). The Holy Spirit was present under the old covenant, but in the new covenant he would be universally given rather than simply being given to prophets, judges, and kings, for instance (Acts 2.17-18). The Spirit would be an abiding, permanent presence in and among God's people rather than sporadically and temporarily coming upon certain individuals (John 14.16). Finally, the chief work of the Spirit would be moral transformation rather than merely empowering people to accomplish a task (Gal 5.22-23). The Spirit came upon Samson repeatedly, but his life was not inwardly changed and sanctified by the Spirit's presence. This new and lasting work of the Spirit could only happen after Christ had atoned for sin then poured out the Spirit as a gift freely offered and received by all God's people. The Spirit is inseparably tied to salvation and to Christ who purchased our salvation at the cross. There would be no Pentecost without Calvary, and Calvary is incomplete without Pentecost. The work of the Son and the gift of the Spirit are both necessary for salvation.[3]

There are *prophecies* from the Old Testament that Jesus fulfilled in the New Testament, which show that he is the promised Messiah, our Savior. Here are some of those prophecies.

- His birth in Bethlehem (Mic 5.2; Matt 2.4-6)

- His flight into Egypt (Hos 11.1; Matt 2.14-15)

- Rejection by his people (Isa 53.3; John 1.11)

- His triumphal entry into Jerusalem (Zech 9.9; Matt 21.1-11)

- He was sold for thirty pieces of silver (Zech 11.12; Matt 26.14-16)

- He was pierced while on the cross (Zech 12.10; John 19.34)

- Soldiers cast lots for his garments (Ps 22.18; Mark 15.24)

- None of his bones were broken (Ps 34.20; John 19.33)

- He was buried with the rich (Isa 53.9; Matt 27.57-60)

- His resurrection from the dead (Ps 16.8-11; Acts 2.24-32)

- His ascension (Ps 68.18; Acts 1.9)

Before Creation

Not only did salvation precede my birth in that God planned to save me before he created the world and promised this salvation in the Old Testament, but salvation also preceded my belief. It preceded my decision to follow Christ. Before I believed in Jesus, God had already chosen me. Ephesians 1.3-4 states, "Blessed be the God and

---

[3] For more on the Holy Spirit, see John Stott, *Baptism & Fullness* (Downers Grove, IL: InterVarsity, 1977); Sinclair B. Ferguson, *The Holy Spirit* (Downers Grove, IL: InterVarsity, 1996); John D. Harvey, *Anointed with the Spirit and Power* (Phillipsburg, NJ: P & R Publishing, 2008).

Father of our Lord Jesus Christ, who has blessed us in Christ with every spiritual blessing in the heavenly places, even as he chose us in him before the foundation of the world, that we should be holy and blameless before him." Ephesians 1.3-14 is one sentence in the Greek, and it details the salvation God has provided for us following a trinitarian outline. The Father chose us (vv. 3-6), the Son redeemed us (vv. 7-12), and the Spirit sealed us (vv. 13-14). The whole Trinity is involved in our salvation.

The Father chose us for salvation. Isn't that a breathtaking thought? We are God's chosen ones, his elect.[4] He wanted us and so he adopted us into his spiritual family (v. 5). Where I pastor, there are three precious girls that were adopted by one of the ladies in the church. Their names are Lexi, Brookie, and Sofia. They needed a family, and this compassionate Christian woman welcomed these girls into her heart and home. They did not adopt their mother; she adopted them. She initiated the process and made the decision. She did this out of love. In the same way, God has adopted us. He chose us before we chose him. We were adopted not because we deserved it or asked to be. We were adopted because it was God's good pleasure to have us in his family.

It's astonishing to look at when and why God chose to save us. *When did he choose us?* In verse 4, Paul says it was before the foundation of the world. It was before we were born or believed in Jesus. This emphasizes the priority of grace. As Charles Spurgeon acknowledged, "I am sure He chose me before I was born, or else He never would have chosen me afterward." *Why did he choose us?* He chose us in order that we would be holy and blameless before him. He didn't choose us because we were holy and blameless but to

---

[4] In the New Testament, Christians are called believers, brothers and sisters, saints, disciples, and a few other names. One of those names is the elect (e.g., Matt 24.22, 24, 31; Luke 18.7; Rom 8.33; Col 3.12; Tit 1.1; Rev 17.14). This title emphasizes that we are God's people and that his people consist of followers of Christ rather than mere descendants of Abraham. It also emphasizes God's initiative and grace in salvation. We are saved, first of all, not because we chose the Lord but because he chose us.

make us so. This reality removes all boasting and gives all glory to God for our salvation. I didn't one day decide to follow Jesus on my own. No, I was awakened by God and drawn to Christ because he had chosen me.

What about those who don't believe? Does God predestine some people to hell? Do we have no choice in our salvation? Scripture is clear that God desires and invites all to be saved and grieves over those who reject his invitation.

- "Do you think that I like to see wicked people die? says the Sovereign LORD. Of course not! I want them to turn from their wicked ways and live" (Ezek 18.23 NLT).

- "Come to me, all who labor and are heavy laden, and I will give you rest" (Matt 11.28).

- "O Jerusalem, Jerusalem, the city that kills the prophets and stones those who are sent to it! How often would I have gathered your children together as a hen gathers her brood under her wings, and you were not willing!" (Matt 23.37).

- "This is good, and it is pleasing in the sight of God our Savior, who desires all people to be saved and to come to the knowledge of the truth" (1 Tim 2.3-4).

- "The Lord is not slow in keeping his promise, as some understand slowness. Instead he is patient with you, not wanting anyone to perish, but everyone to come to repentance" (2 Pet 3.9 NIV).

- "Let the one who is thirsty come; and let the one who wishes take the free gift of the water of life" (Rev 22.17 NIV).

People go to hell because they choose to stay in their sinful condition. Hell was created for the devil and his angels (Matt 25.41). The word "predestine" (*proorizō*) is never used in the New Testament in relation to condemnation (Acts 4.28; Rom 8.29-30; 1 Cor 2.7;

Eph 1.5, 11). Therefore, we cannot blame God if we go to hell.[5] But neither can we praise ourselves if we go to heaven. God is the author and giver of salvation. He chose us, called us, justified us, and one day will glorify us. Did he save us against our will? No, but he did create in us a willing heart that was receptive to the gospel.

Putting all this together is not easy. We attribute our election and salvation completely to God. Yet, we also know that we are responsible for our actions, and unless we believe we will not be saved. Consequently, a certain level of mystery will always accompany the biblical doctrine of election. Maybe that is why the Christian Church has never agreed on the orthodox position on election, as it has, for instance, on the doctrine of the Trinity. What we should be able to agree on is that if we're lost we have no one to blame but ourselves and if we're saved God alone gets the glory. This may be a better path than attempting to overly systematize God's work of salvation in human lives.[6] And regardless, our focus should be on evangelizing the lost and growing in personal holiness. That is the purpose of election. We are chosen to be holy (Eph 1.4; Col 3.12).

The Gospel of Grace

I'd like to end this chapter on the note of grace. Salvation is by God's grace from beginning to end. The gospel is "the gospel of the grace of God" (Acts 20.24). Each one of Paul's letters begins and ends with an emphasis on God's grace and thus our need of it (e.g., Rom 1.7; 16.20). This is also true of our lives. We need grace to commence the Christian life and grace to complete it. Notice the role of God's grace in every aspect of our salvation and walk with the Lord.

- We were *chosen* by grace — "So too at the present time there is a remnant, chosen by grace. But if it is by grace, it is no

---

[5] For more on this issue, see Demarest, *The Cross and Salvation*, 135-38.

[6] Justo L. González, *A Concise History of Christian Doctrine* (Nashville: Abingdon Press, 2005), 107-08.

longer on the basis of works; otherwise grace would no longer be grace" (Rom 11.5-6).

- We *believe* by grace — "When he arrived, he greatly helped those who through grace had believed" (Acts 18.27).

- We are *saved* by grace — "For by grace you have been saved through faith. And this is not your own doing; it is the gift of God" (Eph 2.8).

- We are *justified* by grace — "For all have sinned and fall short of the glory of God, and are justified by his grace as a gift, through the redemption that is in Christ Jesus" (Rom 3.23-24).

- We are *adopted* by grace — "In love he predestined us for adoption to himself as sons through Jesus Christ, according to the purpose of his will to the praise of his glorious grace, with which he has blessed us in the Beloved" (Eph 1.4-6).

- We are *redeemed* by grace — "In him we have redemption through his blood, the forgiveness of our trespasses, according to the riches of his grace" (Eph 1.7).

- We are *sanctified* by grace — "For sin will have no dominion over you, since you are not under law but under grace" (Rom 6.14).

- We are *gifted* by grace — "As each has received a gift, use it to serve one another, as good stewards of God's varied grace" (1 Pet 4.10).

- We *serve* by grace — "But by the grace of God I am what I am, and his grace toward me was not in vain. On the contrary, I worked harder than any of them, though it was not I, but the grace of God that is with me" (1 Cor 15.10).

- We are *strengthened* by grace — "Do not be led away by diverse and strange teachings, for it is good for the heart to be strengthened by grace, not by foods, which have not benefited those devoted to them" (Heb 13.9).

- We are *preserved* by grace — "And now I commend you to God and to the word of his grace, which is able to build you up and to give you the inheritance among all those who are sanctified" (Acts 20.32).

- We will be *perfected* by grace — "Therefore, preparing your minds for action, and being sober-minded, set your hope fully on the grace that will be brought to you at the revelation of Jesus Christ" (1 Pet 1.13).

God's amazing grace! Salvation is by grace from the beginning of our Christian life to the end. God's plan to save us preceded our belief. It preceded our birth. It preceded anyone's birth, for his plan was designed before the creation of the world. This reality magnifies God's grace in our salvation. "Behold, God is my salvation" (Isa 12.2).

CHAPTER TWO

We Can't Save Ourselves

❧❦❧

Recognizing that God is my salvation also means recognizing that I am *not* my salvation. I cannot save myself. I cannot atone for my sin nor free myself from its tenacious grip. There is no such thing as self-salvation in Scripture. Jonah 2.9 emphatically states, "Salvation comes from the LORD" (NIV). The context of this verse in Jonah and in Scripture as a whole shows that this is affirming that salvation comes from the Lord and from him *alone*. There is no other Savior, and thus there is no other provider of salvation. As William Temple once stated, "All is of God; the only thing of my very own which I contribute to my redemption is the sin from which I need to be redeemed."[1]

Wright helpfully explains this reality in the following manner. He writes, "Salvation, as biblically understood, is not at human disposal or a matter of human achievement.

- We do not own or control salvation.

- We cannot dispense salvation to others.

- We certainly cannot sell salvation or offer it on our own terms (though many religions do so—including some perverted forms of Christianity down through the ages).

---

[1] This quote is cited in Wright, *Salvation Belongs to Our God*, 118-19.

- We are not the ones who decide who gets to have salvation, or not.

- We cannot threaten or take away salvation from those to whom God has granted it. It is God's decision and gift, not ours."[2]

This is important to realize, for we will not seek salvation from the Lord until we believe that we need to be saved and that he alone can save us. I remember talking with a man one day and sharing the gospel with him. His objection was that he could not understand how an elderly, godly woman could live for Christ most of her life, while some criminal could pray to be saved just before his death, then both of them would go to the same heaven. He said, "That's just not fair." My response was to explain that the sweet, elderly Christian lady he hypothetically spoke of didn't deserve to go to heaven either. Both of them had sinned against God, and both would be welcomed into heaven by God's grace alone. But that was his stumbling block: God's grace and his need of it. He was a moral man and didn't realize his need of Jesus. And until he does, he will never seek salvation from the Lord. By the way, moral people can be some of the hardest people to reach with the gospel.

We Don't Know We Need to be Saved

When it comes to realizing that we cannot save ourselves, there are a few important truths to keep in mind, three in particular. *First, on our own we don't even know we need to be saved.* This is true of all of us. The Holy Spirit must convict us of our sin and reveal our need of Christ before we will turn to the Lord (John 16.7-11). We think we're okay. Sure, we realize we're not perfect, but at least we're better than our next door neighbor or that jerk at work. Isn't it funny how we like to compare ourselves to people we believe are morally inferior to us? Compared to them, we feel pretty good about ourselves. By the

---

[2] Ibid., 39.

way, is this not one of the chief reasons for our gossip? Talking about other people makes us feel better about ourselves. The problem is that God doesn't compare us to other people; he judges us according to our likeness to him and his law. And that means we all fall short—woefully short!

- "There is no one who does not sin" (1 Kings 8.46).

- "If you, LORD, kept a record of sins, Lord, who could stand?" (Ps 130.3 NIV).

- "Do not bring your servant into judgment, for no one living is righteous before you" (Ps 143.2 NIV).

- "Who can say, 'I have kept my heart pure; I am clean and without sin'?" (Prov 20.9 NIV).

- "Surely there is not a righteous man on earth who does good and never sins" (Eccl 7.20).

- "For all have sinned and fall short of the glory of God" (Rom 3.23).

- "For we all stumble in many ways" (Jam 3.2).

- "If we say we have no sin, we deceive ourselves, and the truth is not in us" (1 John 1.8).

As you can see, the universality of sin is the universal teaching of Scripture. And sin, according to the Westminster Shorter Catechism, is "any want [lack] of conformity unto, or transgression of, the law of God." Sin is when we fail to live up to God's standards or break one of his commands. The universality of sin is one of the main reasons God gave us the law. It was to show us our sin and our corresponding need of salvation. This is the purpose of the law. It leads us to Christ. There are two key mountains in Scripture: Mount Sinai (where Moses received the law) and Mount Calvary (where Jesus died for our sins). We will not come to

Calvary until we first visit Sinai.[3] We must be convicted of our sin
and our powerlessness to atone for our sin and overcome it before
we will feel compelled to turn to Christ for his mercy. As Romans
3.20 explains, "Through the law comes knowledge of sin." Maybe
one of the reasons some professions of faith are shallow and
non-lasting is because these people came to Christ not out of
conviction of sin but simply to have a better life here on earth.
Certainly God can bless us and fill us with joy in this life, but our
main need is forgiveness of sin. We only realize this when we see
our moral bankruptcy in light of God's law. It is God's law that
reveals and breaks our self-righteousness, which is necessary for us
to come to Christ. George Whitefield explains, "You must be made
sick of your righteousness, of all your duties and performances.
There must be a deep conviction before you can be brought out of
your self-righteousness; it is the last idol taken out of our heart."[4]
Has God taken this idol out of your heart, or are you still trusting
in your own righteousness and good behavior to make you
acceptable to God?

We Don't Want to be Saved

Second, on our own we really don't want to be saved. This may
sound ridiculous. Who wouldn't want to be forgiven and go to
heaven? Actually, none of us on our own. The Bible teaches that
we are born into this world with an inbred bent away from God,
even a revulsion towards God. In light of his adulterous scandal,
David acknowledged this painful reality, "Behold, I was brought
forth in iniquity, and in sin did my mother conceive me" (Ps 51.5).
We are not sinners because we sin. Rather, we sin because we are
sinners. Who we are determines what we do. Jesus said, "Every

---

[3] This was made clear to me as I read how elders in the Presbyterian Church of
Scotland would at times ask candidates for church membership, "Have you been to
Sinai?" See Derek W. H. Thomas, *How the Gospel Brings Us All the Way Home*
(Orlando, FL: Reformation Trust, 2011), 60-61.

[4] He made this statement in his sermon, "The Method of Grace," recorded in *Select
Sermons of George Whitefield* (Carlisle, PA: The Banner of Truth Trust, 1990), 83.

healthy tree bears good fruit, but the diseased tree bears bad fruit. A healthy tree cannot bear bad fruit, nor can a diseased tree bear good fruit" (Matt 7.17-18). We are like a diseased tree that bears only rotten fruit. We are sinners from birth, and thus we sin. It is in our nature to do so. The only one who can free us from this propensity to sin is Jesus Christ.

Yet, we don't want Jesus to free us. It takes God's grace to open our hearts and draw us to the Lord for salvation. A beautiful example of this is found in Acts 16. Paul and Silas went to Philippi to preach the gospel, and there they met a business woman named Lydia. She sold purple cloth, which was a lucrative business in that day. She also was religious, for they met her at a prayer service and the text says that she was "a worshiper of God" (v. 14). She believed in God, but was not a follower of Jesus. Consequently, in spite of her money and religion, she still needed salvation. Therefore, they shared the gospel with her and she accepted it. Verse 14 explains how it happened, "The Lord opened her heart to respond to Paul's message" (NIV). Her heart had been closed, but the Lord opened it. He can open your heart too. Unless he does, you will never be saved.

Some put off salvation because they think they can be saved whenever they want. This is a terrible way to live. By delaying salvation we continue to live in our sin which dishonors God and hurts us. Moreover, we can only come to Christ as we are drawn to him from above. Our will is steadfastly set against the Lord. Jesus said, "No one can come to me unless the Father who sent me draws him" (John 6.44). Yes, you can come to Christ whenever you want, but the problem is you never want to without divine intervention. "Therefore, as the Holy Spirit says, 'Today, if you hear his voice, do not harden your hearts'" (Heb 3.7-8). Don't delay. Place your faith in Christ today and be saved.

We Can't Save Ourselves

Third, on our own we're not able to save ourselves. Even if on our own we knew our need of salvation and desired it (neither of which is true), we still could not procure salvation for ourselves. Yet, many try.

They try to save themselves by their morality or their religion. But we can never be good enough or religious enough to save ourselves. If we could save ourselves by being good, then let me ask you two questions. How good is good enough, and why did Jesus die on the cross? Salvation by our good works requires perfect obedience to God's law (Gal 3.10; 5.3; Jam 2.10), a feat which we are unable to attain. In his final sermon before dying, Whitefield categorically denounced this possibility. He exclaimed, "Works! Works! A man get to heaven by works! I would as soon think of climbing to the moon on a rope of sand!"[5] We couldn't climb a small hill with a rope of sand, let alone reach the moon.

We can never be good enough to deserve salvation. And if we could, then Jesus's death was a colossal mistake. He died for our sins because there was no other way for us to be forgiven and restored to a right relationship with God. Paul explains, "I do not treat the grace of God as meaningless. For if keeping the law could make us right with God, then there was no need for Christ to die" (Gal 2.21 NLT). Christ died to save us because we could not save ourselves. Our good deeds could never atone for our sin. Good deeds do not have the power to cancel out bad deeds, and even our good deeds need God's mercy, for they are not perfectly good in his sight.

There is a great example of this in the life of David Dickson, a Scottish minister and theologian from the seventeenth century. He was a very godly man, but when he became sick and knew that he would die, he told a friend, "I have taken all my good deeds, and all my bad deeds, and have cast them together in a heap before the Lord, and have fled from both to Jesus Christ, and in Him I have sweet peace."[6] Whether coming to the Lord for salvation or to commune with him as a believer, this should always be our attitude. We are saved by the name of the Lord, and we pray in his name (Acts 2.21; John 14.13). The power and merits of his name are our only hope.

---

[5] Luke Tyerman, *The Life of the Rev. George Whitefield*, 2 vols. (New York: Anson D. F. Randolph, 1877), 2.596.

[6] Thomas, *How the Gospel Brings Us All the Way Home*, 123.

Therefore, we see that our morality can never save us, neither can our religion. This is the fallacy of pluralism. All religions are not equal, and actually no religion can provide salvation. Michael Green writes, "Far from all religions leading to God, *no* religion can lead to God...We do not need a religion, but a revelation. And that is precisely what Christianity claims to be."[7] Christianity is not another religion, at least it is not intended to be. Rather, it is a group of people who have been transformed by the unique revelation of Jesus Christ and his saving power. No religion can save us, but a relationship with Jesus Christ can. Jesus said, "I am the way, and the truth, and the life. No one comes to the Father except through me" (John 14.6). Salvation is found in him alone.

The Holy Club was a religious small group started by Charles Wesley while he attended Oxford University. It was later led by his older brother John Wesley. Whitefield was also a member of this group. These and other men met regularly to fast and pray, to study the Greek New Testament, to do good works, and to examine their lives before God. The name of the group was not self-chosen. Other students made fun of them by calling them the Holy Club. They were also called Methodists which became the name of the church associated with John Wesley. The remarkable thing is that these men were not born again. They were extremely religious yet unsaved. They were seeking God's acceptance by works rather than by grace. Later all three would experience the new birth and begin preaching salvation by grace alone. They learned that we're not saved by our attempts to be holy; rather, we're saved by the merits of Christ received by faith alone.

One of the main reasons our morality and religion cannot save us is because of our sin. Nothing good we do can atone for past sins; plus, sin continues to cling to even the best attempts to be moral or religious. The only thing that can atone for sin is the blood of Christ. "Without the shedding of blood there is no forgiveness of sins" (Heb

---

[7] Michael Green, *"But Don't All Religions Lead to God?"* (Grand Rapids, MI: Baker Books, 2002), 23.

9.22). And the only way to please God by our service is to do it with faith in Christ. Only then is our service "acceptable to God through Jesus Christ" (1 Pet 2.5).

Images of Sin

The Bible describes sin with a number of different images, and each of these images underscores our inability to remove sin ourselves.

- Sin is like a *stain* too deep to remove. "Though you wash yourself with lye and use much soap, the stain of your guilt is still before me, declares the Lord GOD" (Jer 2.22).

- Sin is like a *debt* too great to repay. "Forgive us our debts, as we also have forgiven our debtors" (Matt 6.12).

- Sin is like a *burden* too heavy to bear. "For my iniquities have gone over my head; they weigh like a burden too heavy for me" (Ps 38.4 NRSV).

- Sin is like a *prison* too secure to escape. "But scripture has declared the whole world to be prisoners in subjection to sin, so that faith in Jesus Christ should be the ground on which the promised blessing is given to those who believe" (Gal 3.22 REB).

Our sin is compared to a deep stain, an unrepayable debt, an overwhelming burden, and an inescapable prison. On our own we cannot wash away the stain, pay back the debt, lift the burden, or escape the prison cell. On our own we are helpless and hopeless. Morality is not a Savior, nor is religion. We need a Savior beyond ourselves who will meet us where we are. We need a divine Savior to come to us, for we could never reach him in our strength.

E. Stanley Jones gives us an illustration of how God has done this through his Son, the Lord Jesus Christ.[8] He points out how many try to reach God by climbing a ladder to heaven, climbing rung

---

[8] E. Stanley Jones, *Christian Maturity* (Nashville: Abingdon Press, 1957), 22.

by rung by their religion, good works, and self-effort. But it's impossible. The ladder is too high. The good news is that God has graciously climbed down the ladder from heaven to earth in the person of Jesus Christ. He came to us when we couldn't reach him. "The Word became flesh and dwelt among us" (John 1.14). That's the gospel! God took on human flesh to live among us and die for us. It's time to explore a little more fully how God has purchased our salvation through the work of his Son.

CHAPTER THREE

Salvation through Jesus Christ

❧

So far we have learned that God planned to save us before we were born, even before creation, and that we cannot save ourselves. Let's now look at how salvation has been provided for us in the work of Jesus Christ.

Jesus Christ can save us because of who he is and what he has done. This speaks of the person and work of Christ. The two are inseparable.[1] The work of Christ for our salvation is only effective because of his person. If Christ was not who he said he was, then his death would have no meaning or power. Consequently, it is necessary to deal with his person before we look at his work.

---

[1] This does not mean that it is inappropriate to deal with the person and work of Christ separately; it just means that these two subjects will always overlap. For two helpful books on these subjects, see Donald Macleod, *The Person of Christ* (Downers Grove, IL: InterVarsity, 1998); Robert Letham, *The Work of Christ* (Downers Grove, IL: InterVarsity, 1993). For a book that looks at both the person and work of Christ, see Stephen Wellum, *Christ Alone: The Uniqueness of Jesus as Savior* (Grand Rapids, MI: Zondervan, 2017).

The Person of Christ

There are certain truths that we accept as Christians that are difficult to understand, but we accept them by faith. We believe there is one God revealed in three persons—Father, Son, and Holy Spirit. This is not three gods, but one God eternally existent in three persons. We believe Scripture is God's inspired word, though it was written by human beings. We believe God preserved these fallible men and led them to write what he wanted so that the Bible they left us is fully trustworthy and authoritative concerning what we believe and how we live.[2] We believe God is sovereign, but we also believe that human beings are not robots and will be held accountable for their actions. And concerning Jesus, we believe he is fully God and fully man at the same time. He possesses full deity and full humanity. He is one person, but he has two natures—a divine nature and a human nature. This is the teaching of Scripture (John 1.1, 14; Col 2.9). It was explained, affirmed, and pronounced as orthodoxy at the Council of Chalcedon in AD 451.

Without such a Savior—one who is both divine and human, there would be no salvation. John Calvin explains, "Finally, since as God alone he could not suffer and as man alone he could not conquer death, he combined the human nature with the divine. Then he could subject the weakness of the human to death, for an expiation of sin, and by the power of the divine could achieve for us victory over death. So those who rob Christ of divinity or humanity either detract from his glory or obscure his goodness. They hurt men too, undermining their faith which cannot stand without this foundation."[3] A solely divine Savior could not have died for our sins. A solely human Savior could not be a perfect sacrifice or overcome

---

[2] For two excellent books on the inspiration and trustworthiness of Scripture, see J. I. Packer, *"Fundamentalism" and the Word of God* (Grand Rapids, MI: Eerdmans, 1958); Ben Witherington III, *The Living Word of God* (Waco, TX: Baylor University Press, 2009).

[3] John Calvin, *The Institutes of Christian Religion*, ed. Tony Lane and Hilary Osborne (Grand Rapids, MI: Baker Academic, 1987), 2.12.3.

death. But a Savior who is both divine and human could provide redemption for us, and he has.

When we say that we believe that Jesus is both fully God and fully man, that is what we mean. He was not 50% divine and 50% human; rather, he was 100% both. He did not set aside his deity in order to become human. To the contrary, while remaining divine, he took on human flesh so that he could live among us and die for us. In the early church, some could not accept this. An ancient heresy known as *docetism* taught that Jesus seemed to be human but was really only divine.[4] But Jesus was truly human. Here are some examples of his full humanity.

- *Jesus was born of a woman (Luke 2.7; Gal 4.4).* His conception was supernatural, but his growth in the womb and his birth were natural.

- *Jesus grew physically and intellectually (Luke 2.40, 52).* In his human nature, he grew and developed like a normal child.

- *Jesus became hungry and thirsty (Mark 11.12; John 19.28).* He had to eat food and drink liquids to survive as a human being.

- *Jesus became tired and slept (Mark 4.38; John 4.6).* His body got weary and he had to sleep at night to refresh himself.

- *Jesus was tempted (Matt 4.1-11; Heb 4.15).* Jesus never sinned, but he was tempted severely at times.

- *Jesus died (Matt 27.50).* On the cross he truly died.

As you can see, Jesus was a human being. Yet, he never sinned. The sinlessness of Christ is the consistent teaching of the New

---

[4] This heresy gets its name from the Greek word *dokeō*, which means "to seem or appear." Proponents of this heresy wrongly believed that the human body was evil in and of itself, and thus for Jesus to be human meant that he could not be sinless or divine.

Testament, even being taught by those who knew him intimately while on earth, namely, Peter and John (2 Cor 5.21; Heb 4.15; 1 Pet. 2.22; 1 John 3.5). How then could he be fully human? This is because sin is not natural to humanity. The first couple was created without sin, yet they were fully human. If anything, sin makes us less human. It dehumanizes us. That's why we refer to atrocious acts as inhumane. Thus, Jesus could be human and was human, even though he was also without sin.

Scripture also teaches the full deity of Christ. We see this in Jesus's divine titles, divine attributes, and divine actions. Let's begin with his titles. The following titles express his divine status.

Divine Titles

Jesus is *Lord* (Rom 10.9-13). In the Roman Empire, the title "Lord" was used of the emperor to speak of him as divine. It was also used in the Old Testament to refer to God. The Septuagint (the Greek Old Testament) translated Yahweh with the word *kurios* ("Lord"). Some English translations put this word in all caps when this is done, thus translating it as "LORD." At times Old Testament quotations that speak of Yahweh are ascribed to Jesus, as in this Romans 10 passage which cites Joel 2.32 in relation to Jesus. Therefore, to say Jesus is Lord is to say he is divine.

Jesus is the *Son of God* (Matt 14.33; 1 John 4.15). This does not speak of a biological birth. Rather, Jesus is the Son of God in the sense that he shares the same nature as God the Father and was sent by him to carry out his will. We are sons of God by adoption; Jesus is the Son of God by nature. He is the Son of God in a unique way (John 3.16).

Jesus is *God*. Eight times in the New Testament Jesus is specifically referred to as "God."

- "In the beginning was the Word, and the Word was with God, and the Word was God" (John 1.1).

- "No one has ever seen God; the only God, who is at the Father's side, he has made him known" (John 1.18).

- "Thomas answered him, 'My Lord and my God!'" (John 20.28).

- "To them belong the patriarchs, and from their race, according to the flesh, is the Christ, who is God over all, blessed forever. Amen" (Rom 9.5).

- "Waiting for our blessed hope, the appearing of the glory of our great God and Savior Jesus Christ" (Tit 2.13).

- "But of the Son he says, 'Your throne, O God, is forever and ever, the scepter of uprightness is the scepter of your kingdom'" (Heb 1.8).

- "Simeon Peter, a servant and an apostle of Jesus Christ: To those who have received a faith equal to ours through the righteousness of our God and Savior Jesus Christ" (2 Pet 1.1 CSB).

- "And we know that the Son of God has come and has given us understanding, so that we may know him who is true; and we are in him who is true, in his Son Jesus Christ. He is the true God and eternal life" (1 John 5.20).

This is incredible in light of the following: it was said in a strictly monotheistic context (Deut 6.4; Mark 12.29), four different New Testament authors asserted this (John, Paul, Peter, and the author of Hebrews), and it was said almost in passing. It is simply poor scholarship to assert that Jesus's deity was a later development in the church. His deity was affirmed in the New Testament, which was written during the first century.

Divine Attributes

Divine attributes are characteristics that belong to God. Some attributes are communicable, which means we as humans can share in them as they are imparted to us by God. An example would be God's holiness. This is an attribute of God, but we too can be holy. We are actually commanded to be holy (1 Pet 1.15-16). Other attributes are non-communicable, which means they belong uniquely to God and cannot be transferred to others. Jesus possessed both types of attributes, revealing that he is God. Here are three examples of non-communicable attributes that he had.

Jesus is *omnipotent* (all-powerful). "And Jesus came and said to them, 'All authority in heaven and on earth has been given to me'" (Matt 28.18). No human or angel could legitimately make this claim, but Jesus did. He possesses complete, universal authority in heaven and on earth. This declaration is followed by the baptismal formula that places the Son on the same level with the Father (v. 19).

Jesus is *omnipresent* (present everywhere). "And behold, I am with you always, to the end of the age" (Matt 28.20). Jesus's presence can be with believers around the world as they gather on the Lord's Day. How? Because he is omnipresent.

Jesus is *omniscient* (all-knowing). "And they prayed and said, 'You, Lord, who know the hearts of all, show which one of these two you have chosen'" (Acts 1.24). This is a prayer to the Lord Jesus, which reveals his divine status in how he is described and that prayer is offered to him in the first place. The ability to read hearts is a characteristic of divinity. We see people's outward life, but only God can read the human heart (1 Sam 16.7).

Divine Actions

Finally, we see Jesus's divine status in actions that he performed or will perform. Jesus did things that only God can do or should do. By his actions Jesus proved that he was divine.

Jesus *forgave sins* (Luke 5.17-26; 7.48-50). He didn't simply forgive people's sins on behalf of God. He forgave sins in his own name and by his own authority. "The Son of Man has authority on earth to forgive sins" (Luke 5.24). It would be blasphemy to claim this ability unless one was God, as the religious leaders certainly knew (v. 21).

Jesus *raised the dead* (Matt 11.5; John 5.21, 25-26; 11.25). He raised the widow's son from Nain (Luke 7.11-17), Jairus's daughter

(Mark 5.21-24, 35-43), and Lazarus (John 11). It is true that other individuals raised people from the dead, such as Elijah (1 Kings 17.17-24) and Elisha (2 Kings 4.8-37). However, they did so not in their own power, but by imploring God to raise them. Jesus, on the other hand, had the power himself to raise people from the dead. He raised people by virtue of his own authority and Godhead. That's why he is appropriately called "the Author of life" (Acts 3.15).

Jesus *willingly received worship* (Matt 14.33; 28.9, 17; Heb 1.6). This is amazing when you contrast this with other instances in the New Testament where people attempted to worship a human being. When Cornelius fell at Peter's feet in worship, he told him to get up for he was only a man (Acts 10.25-26). When the people declared that Herod spoke as God, he was struck down for not denying this (Acts 12.20-23). When the people of Lystra attempted to sacrifice to Paul and Barnabas as gods, they tore their clothes in great displeasure (Acts 14.8-18). Yet, Jesus willingly accepted worship. Either he was an egomaniac or he was God.

Jesus *will judge the world* (Matt 25.31-46). No one is perfect enough or powerful enough to judge the world except God. Thus, Jesus's deity is revealed in that he will serve as universal judge. John 5.22 states, "For the Father judges no one, but has given all judgment to the Son."

The Work of Christ

Now that we have looked at who Jesus is, it is time to investigate what he has done to save us. Paul writes, "For I delivered to you as of first importance what I also received: that Christ died for our sins in accordance with the Scriptures, that he was buried, that he was raised on the third day in accordance with the Scriptures" (1 Cor 15.3-4). There are many teachings in the Bible, but the gospel is "of first importance." There are primary doctrines and secondary doctrines.[5]

---

[5] A few examples of secondary doctrines would be the mode of baptism, one's view on speaking in tongues, and how one understands the millennium. It is not that these teachings are unimportant. It's just that they are not salvation doctrines. You can be saved even if you believe incorrectly about these issues.

The gospel is definitely a primary doctrine, if not *the* primary doctrine. The gospel or good news is that Christ, who is both fully God and fully human, died for our sins and was raised from the dead on the third day. The gospel is not trying to be like Jesus or even the new birth. The gospel is what Christ did at the cross and resurrection to purchase our salvation. The new birth is the result of the gospel being active in a person's life, but the gospel itself is what Christ has done to atone for our sin.

It is clear from Scripture that there would be no salvation from sin without the death of Christ. But how is his death connected to our salvation? Why did he die? Actually, Jesus died for a number of reasons. *He died to prove God's love for us.* Romans 5.8 states, "But God proves his own love for us in that while we were still sinners, Christ died for us" (CSB). How can we ever doubt God's eternal, unconditional love for us when we look at the cross? God loved us so much that he gave his best, his only Son, to die for us. God assures us of his love objectively through the cross and subjectively or internally through the work of his Spirit who indwells us as believers (Rom 5.5). We have no reason to doubt God's love. He proved his love and he poured his love into our hearts. Thank God for his incredible love!

Jesus also died to leave us an example of servanthood. "For to this you have been called, because Christ also suffered for you, leaving you an example, so that you might follow in his steps" (1 Pet 2.21). We too are to take up our cross and follow Jesus, which may involve martyrdom but will certainly involve dying to our selfish ambition (Luke 9.23). We cannot follow the crucified one if we're not willing to die ourselves. His death showed us how to live.

Most importantly, Jesus died as an atoning sacrifice to endure God's wrath so that we can be forgiven of our sin and reconciled to the Father. Here are a number of verses that emphasize that Jesus died in our place to atone for our sin and reconcile us to God.[6]

---

[6] For more on the atoning, substitutionary death of Jesus, see Steve Jeffery, Michael Ovey, and Andrew Sach, *Pierced for Our Transgressions* (Wheaton, IL: Crossway, 2007).

- "But he was pierced for our transgressions; he was crushed for our iniquities; upon him was the chastisement that brought us peace, and with his wounds we are healed. All we like sheep have gone astray; we have turned—every one—to his own way; and the LORD has laid on him the iniquity of us all" (Isa 53.5-6).

- "For even the Son of Man came not to be served but to serve, and to give his life as a ransom for many" (Mark 10.45).

- "For while we were still weak, at the right time Christ died for the ungodly" (Rom 5.6).

- "For our sake he made him to be sin who knew no sin, so that in him we might become the righteousness of God" (2 Cor 5.21).

- "Christ redeemed us from the curse of the law by becoming a curse for us—for it is written, 'Cursed is everyone who is hanged on a tree'" (Gal 3.13).

- "And you, who were dead in your trespasses and the uncircumcision of your flesh, God made alive together with him, having forgiven us all our trespasses, by canceling the record of debt that stood against us with its legal demands. This he set aside, nailing it to the cross" (Col 2.13-14).

- "For there is one God, and there is one mediator between God and men, the man Christ Jesus, who gave himself as a ransom for all" (1 Tim 2.5-6).

- "He it is who gave himself for us that he might redeem us from all iniquity and purify for himself a people of his own who are zealous for good deeds" (Tit 2.14 NRSV).

- "He himself bore our sins in his body on the tree, that we might die to sin and live to righteousness" (1 Pet 2.24).

- "For Christ also suffered once for sins, the righteous for the unrighteous, that he might bring us to God, being put to death in the flesh but made alive in the spirit" (1 Pet 3.18).

- "He is the propitiation for our sins, and not for ours only but also for the sins of the whole world" (1 John 2.2).[7]

Our sins deserve the wrath and judgment of God. Romans 6.23 teaches us that "the wages of sin is death." What we deserve for our sin is death, and not just physical death but eternal death—eternal separation from God in hell. The good news is that Jesus died in our place. He bore God's wrath on our behalf. He became "a curse for us" (Gal 3.13), which means that the curse or judgment we deserve for breaking God's law was endured by him on our behalf. He was made sin (2 Cor 5.21), which means he was treated by God as if he had committed the sins that we are guilty of. He became a sacrifice for our sins. He died an atoning, substitutionary death. We deserved to die and face God's judgment, but he died in our place.

While on the cross, the religious leaders mocked Jesus saying, "He saved others; he cannot save himself" (Mark 15.31). But the truth is had he saved himself, he could not have saved us. He saved us by not saving himself. He drank the cup of God's wrath for us (Mark 14.36; Isa 51.17). While dying, darkness covered the land, which was a sign of God's judgment (Mark 15.33; Exod 10.21-23). It signified God's judgment, possibly on those who crucified his Son but certainly on Jesus himself. That is why he agonized to face death as he prayed in Gethsemane (Mark 14.32-42), and why he cried out from the cross, "My God, my God, why have you forsaken me?" (Mark 15.34). He was forsaken because God treated him as the epitome of sin so that he could forgive us and never forsake us as he did his Son on the cross (Matt 28.20; Heb 13.5).[8]

---

[7] A propitiation is a sacrifice or offering that turns aside God's wrath. It appeases his wrath so that we experience his favor and acceptance rather than his judgment.

[8] For more on the relation between Jesus's death and God's wrath, see Peter G. Bolt, *The Cross from a Distance* (Downers Grove, IL: InterVarsity, 2004). This is an

The death of Christ is critical to our salvation, but his death without his resurrection would be powerless. It is the death and resurrection of Christ that saves us. A dead Savior is no Savior at all. The resurrection revealed that Jesus was indeed the Son of God and that his sacrifice was accepted by God the Father. Had he been an imposter or had his death not been atoning, God would have left him in the tomb. The resurrection is our guarantee that Jesus's death does actually save. He was "raised for our justification" (Rom 4.25). R. Albert Mohler explains, "The resurrection is just as indispensable as Christ's death. Without the resurrection of Christ, we can have no confidence that God accepted Christ's sacrifice. Without the resurrection of Christ, we can have no confidence that the new creation has dawned and will one day come in fullness. Without the resurrection of Christ and his ascension, we can have no confidence that he is interceding for us at the Father's right hand."[9] Similarly, Donald Macleod states, "The resurrection gives coherence to the entire New Testament: to the story of the virgin birth, to the miracles, to the transfiguration, to the titles ascribed to Jesus, to the worship accorded him, to Pentecost, to the idea of 'en Christo', to the perception of his death as an atoning sacrifice, to the expectation of the parousia, to the hope of resurrection and to the belief in a final judgment."[10] As Paul affirms in 1 Corinthians 15.3-4, the gospel entails both the death and resurrection of Christ.

Concerning the resurrection of Christ, it's important to affirm the historicity of his resurrection. Christ didn't simply rise in a spiritual or mystical way. He actually defeated death and came out of the tomb on the third day to live forevermore. His resurrection was bodily. The resurrected Jesus invited his disciples to touch him, and

---

excellent monograph on the atoning death of Jesus in Mark's Gospel. It helped solidify in my mind that Mark's Gospel presents Jesus's death as an atoning sacrifice that appeased God's wrath.

[9] R. Albert Mohler, *Acts 1-12 For You* (Purcellville, VA: The Good Book Company, 2018), 23-24.

[10] Macleod, *The Person of Christ*, 237.

he even ate fish in their presence (Luke 24.36-43). His resurrection was also historically verified. Over five hundred witnesses saw the risen Lord (1 Cor 15.6), and many of them suffered and some even gave their life for this belief. In light of this, I am firmly persuaded and believe wholeheartedly in the bodily resurrection of Christ. But not everyone does.

While I was pursuing my master's degree at the Southern Baptist Theological Seminary, I worked at UPS for a few years. The first few days on the job I was trained by a young man named John. He was a very nice and personable fellow. After a day or two of training, I told him I was a Christian. He claimed to be a Christian too.

One night while being trained by John, we began talking about the Bible and whether we can trust the Bible. I told him that I believed that Scripture is fully inspired and trustworthy. He questioned my conviction. He said, "Surely you don't believe that Jonah was swallowed by a whale, do you?" I explained to him that it is not clear in Scripture that it was actually a whale. The Bible simply says it was a very large fish. But I also told him that I did believe it. I then asked if he believed that God created the world. He responded, "Of course, I do." I replied, "Which is easier, to create this world out of nothing or to preserve a man alive in the belly of a big fish?" I then told him that once we believe in creation the other miracles shouldn't be that difficult for us to believe.

I decided to press John a little more. I asked, "Do you believe that God raised Jesus Christ from the dead?" He claimed that he did. Therefore, I said, "You're telling me that you believe that God raised a man from the dead, but you can't believe in the story about Jonah." He immediately saw his inconsistency. He then started to backtrack, saying that he didn't believe that God literally raised Jesus from the dead. That's when I explained to him that you can't be a Christian unless you believe in the bodily resurrection of Jesus. Romans 10.9 plainly states, "If you confess with your mouth that Jesus is Lord and believe in your heart that God raised him from the dead, you will be saved." The historical, bodily resurrection of Christ is central to salvation and necessary to believe to be saved.

So, Jesus lived a sinless life, died for our sins, and rose again on the third day. But now he is at God's right hand interceding for us. The intercession of Christ is also connected to our salvation, particularly its preservation. Paul states, "Who then is the one who condemns? No one. Christ Jesus who died—more than that, who was raised to life—is at the right hand of God and is also interceding for us" (Rom 8.34 NIV). The climactic reason why we do not have to fear God's condemnation is because Jesus is interceding for us at God's right hand. His intercession is based on his death and resurrection and is effective because of who he is and where he sits. The right hand is a place of honor and power. At God's right hand, Jesus prays for us and intercedes on our behalf. This is a precious truth revealed in Scripture.

- "Simon, Simon, Satan has asked to sift all of you as wheat. But I have prayed for you, Simon, that your faith may not fail. And when you have turned back, strengthen your brothers" (Luke 22.31-32 NIV).

- "I am praying for them. I am not praying for the world but for those whom you have given me, for they are yours. All mine are yours, and yours are mine, and I am glorified in them. And I am no longer in the world, but they are in the world, and I am coming to you. Holy Father, keep them in your name, which you have given me, that they may be one, even as we are one. While I was with them, I kept them in your name, which you have given me. I have guarded them, and not one of them has been lost except the son of destruction, that the Scripture might be fulfilled. But now I am coming to you, and these things I speak in the world, that they may have my joy fulfilled in themselves. I have given them your word, and the world has hated them because they are not of the world, just as I am not of the world. I do not ask that you take them out of the world, but that you keep them from the evil one" (John 17.9-15).

- "For there is one God, and there is one mediator between God and men, the man Christ Jesus" (1 Tim 2.5).

- "Consequently, he is able to save to the uttermost those who draw near to God through him, since he always lives to make intercession for them" (Heb 7.25).

- "My little children, I am writing these things to you so that you may not sin. But if anyone does sin, we have an advocate with the Father, Jesus Christ the righteous. He is the propitiation for our sins, and not for ours only but also for the sins of the whole world" (1 John 2.1-2).

Jesus is our mediator, our intercessor, our advocate. A mediator is a peacemaker, one who reconciles two parties that are at odds. An intercessor appeals, on behalf of another, to someone who has the power to rectify an unfavorable situation. An advocate is like a defending attorney, one who stands at our side and pleads our cause. As mediator, Jesus's blood covers our sin and appeases God's wrath. As intercessor and advocate, Jesus pleads the merits of his death before the Father so that we are accepted by God in spite of the sins we have committed. Because of Jesus, God is for us; he is not against us (Rom 8.31). This does not mean that Jesus persuades God the Father against his will to show us mercy. Remember, it was the Father who sent Jesus to die for us (John 3.16; Gal 1.4; 1 John 4.10). Salvation was God's plan before the creation of the world. And in the plan of God, Jesus's death provided the Father a way to forgive and accept us in spite of our sins without injuring his justice or holiness.

The work of Christ to save us also includes his glorious return. We learned earlier that salvation is past, present, and future. We have been saved, we are being saved, and we will be saved in the future. When Christ returns, he will finalize the salvation he won for us. That is why the day of judgment for believers is called "the day of redemption" (Eph 4.30). It is not a day to dread but a day to delight in. On that day we will be fully redeemed. Then we will receive a new, immortal body and live forever in the presence of the Lord.

Then there will be no sin, no Satan, no sickness, and no separation from believing loved ones. Salvation will be complete. What a day that will be!

As we conclude this chapter on the work of Christ in salvation, it's important to reemphasize that salvation is found in him alone. There are not multiple ways or paths to God. Jesus is the only way to the Father, and the one and only mediator between God and humanity (John 14.6; 1 Tim 2.5). Some scoff at this notion, pointing out that there are sincere, moral people found in the various religions of the world. Salvation, however, is not principally about being sincere or good; it is about being forgiven and freed from sin. Only Christ can do this for us. He alone is Savior. Have you received Christ as your Savior? In this next chapter, I will explain how you can receive salvation through faith in Christ alone.

CHAPTER FOUR

Faith in Jesus Christ

❦

We have looked at the salvation Jesus has provided for us, but this salvation will not benefit us unless we receive it for ourselves. The way we receive salvation is by faith in Jesus Christ. Though the work of Christ is the basis of our salvation, faith is the means by which we receive it. Scripture makes this abundantly clear.

- "And when Jesus saw their *faith*, he said to the paralytic, 'Take heart, my son; your sins are forgiven'" (Matt 9.2).[1]

- "And he said to the woman, 'Your *faith* has saved you; go in peace'" (Luke 7.50).

- "But to all who did receive him, who *believed* in his name, he gave the right to become children of God" (John 1.12).

- "For God so loved the world, that he gave his only Son, that whoever *believes* in him should not perish but have eternal life" (John 3.16).

---

[1] The text reads "their faith." Though this includes the faith of his friends who carried him, there is no reason why it does not also refer to the paralytic's faith. The italics in all these verses on salvation by faith were added.

- "Truly, truly, I say to you, whoever *believes* has eternal life" (John 6.47).

- "To him all the prophets bear witness that everyone who *believes* in him receives forgiveness of sins through his name" (Acts 10.43).

- "Then he brought them out and said, 'Sirs, what must I do to be saved?' And they said, '*Believe* in the Lord Jesus, and you will be saved, you and your household'" (Acts 16.30-31).

- "If you confess with your mouth that Jesus is Lord and *believe* in your heart that God raised him from the dead, you will be saved" (Rom 10.9).

- "For since, in the wisdom of God, the world did not know God through wisdom, it pleased God through the folly of what we preach to save those who *believe*" (1 Cor 1.21).

- "For by grace you have been saved through *faith*" (Eph 2.8).

- "For to this end we toil and strive, because we have our hope set on the living God, who is the Savior of all people, especially of those who *believe*" (1 Tim 4.10).

- "Though you do not now see him, you *believe* in him and rejoice with joy that is inexpressible and filled with glory, obtaining the outcome of your *faith*, the salvation of your souls" (1 Pet 1.8-9).

What Saving Faith is Not

As is clear from these verses, we are saved by faith, but not just any faith. We are saved by faith in Jesus Christ. It might be helpful to point out what type of faith does *not* save us. The following are things we can believe in without being saved.

It is not enough to believe in the existence of God. We should believe that God exists. Creation itself testifies to the existence of an all-powerful God (Ps 19.1; Rom 1.18-20). We should believe in God's existence, but that is not enough to save us. James 2.19 states, "You believe that God is one; you do well. Even the demons believe—and shudder!" Demons believe in God's existence and power, but they are not saved, and neither are we for simply believing that God exists. Just because you're not an atheist doesn't mean you're a Christian.

It is not enough to believe in your church or your pastor. I hope you attend a biblically-based, Christ-centered church, and I hope you have a good pastor, but neither can save you. Attending church is not the same as being a Christian. Plus, we are not to build our life around a pastor or an evangelist. We are to build our life around Jesus Christ. If you are a Christian, you will want to attend church and listen to your pastor's sermons. But without salvation, church attendance and liking your pastor are not enough. Scripture teaches us to place our faith in Jesus, not in his people or his servants.

It is not enough to believe that Jesus was a teacher or a prophet. He was both, but he was also more than both. A teacher can instruct and a prophet can predict, but the Son of God can actually save. Muslims believe that Jesus was a prophet. He is mentioned various times in the Koran. But they do not believe that Jesus is the Son of God. They respect Jesus, but they do not worship him. We cannot simply believe that Jesus was a teacher or a prophet and be forgiven of our sins. Unless Jesus died for our sins and was resurrected as the Son of God, there is no forgiveness.

It is not enough to believe conceptually that Jesus is the Messiah. We are not talking about head knowledge or merely agreeing with the statement that Jesus is the Messiah. This belief must come from the heart and be planted there by God. We see this in the case of Peter. Jesus asked him who he thought he was. Peter said, "You are the Christ, the Son of the living God." Jesus responded, "Blessed are you, Simon Bar-Jonah! For flesh and blood has not revealed this to you, but my Father who is in heaven" (Matt 16.17). His confession was more than words or mental assent. It was a God-given, God-revealed confession. Similarly, Paul says that the confession "Jesus is Lord" must come from the heart and be inspired by the Holy Spirit for us to be saved (Rom 10.9; 1 Cor 12.3).

Sola Fide

If these are things that are not enough to believe in to be saved, what is saving faith? True, saving faith is relying on Jesus alone for salvation. It is believing that Jesus's death atoned for our sin and that through him we can be forgiven and reconciled to God. Calvin defines saving faith in this way: "We shall have a complete definition of faith if we say that it is a firm and sure knowledge of the divine favour towards us, founded on the truth of a free promise in Christ, revealed to our minds and sealed on our hearts by the Holy Spirit."[2] John Newton, the author of the famous hymn "Amazing Grace," states, "This is faith: a renouncing of everything we are apt to call our own and relying wholly upon the blood, righteousness and intercession of Jesus." Saving faith is personal faith. John Wesley testifies of the personal faith that God gave him when he was converted, "I felt my heart strangely warmed. I felt I did trust in Christ, Christ alone for salvation; and an assurance was given me that he had taken away *my* sins, even *mine*, and saved *me* from the law of sin and death."[3] Before his conversion, Wesley had acknowledged that Christ was the Savior of the world, but now he could say that Christ was his Savior, his personal Savior. Do you know Christ as your personal Savior?

Saving faith is not only personal; it is sufficient in terms of being the means of salvation. The Bible teaches that we are saved by faith alone, what the Protestant Reformers referred to as *sola fide*. We are not saved by good deeds or even by faith and good deeds, but by faith alone. This was the experience of the patriarch Abraham (Gen 15.1-6). God promised him innumerable descendants when he had

---

[2] Calvin, *The Institutes of Christian Religion*, 3.2.7.

[3] The italics were added by Wesley himself in his journal entry on May 24, 1738. For an insightful, enjoyable biography of Wesley, see Stephen Tomkins, *John Wesley: A Biography* (Grand Rapids, MI: Eerdmans, 2003).

none and when he and his wife were up in age. All he could do was believe, and that was enough. Verse 6 states, "And he believed the LORD, and he counted it to him as righteousness." He was given a righteous status before the Lord through faith. Righteousness was counted or imputed to his account.[4] He had not been circumcised yet, nor had the Ten Commandments been given. But he believed, and therefore he was righteous in God's sight.

The sinful woman who anointed Jesus's feet with her tears and wiped his feet with her hair was saved by faith alone (Luke 7.36-50). Jesus said to her, "Your faith has saved you; go in peace" (v. 50). He didn't say, "Your tears have saved you" or "Your love has saved you" or even "Your faith and love have saved you." Rather, he simply said, "Your faith has saved you; go in peace." She was saved by faith in Christ alone. That is why she could depart in peace. There is no peace without *sola fide*. Peace is the result of the free and full forgiveness offered to us as a gift, which is received by faith alone. If I'm always wondering if I've done enough to be saved, then there's no peace. But if I know that Christ did it all and I receive his salvation by faith, then I can have true peace and lasting assurance.

The criminal who was crucified next to Jesus entered paradise by faith alone (Luke 23.39-43). Unlike the other criminal, he recognized who Jesus was and asked for mercy.[5] Jesus responded with these words, "Truly, I say to you, today you will be with me in paradise" (v. 43). By the way, this teaches that when we die as believers we go immediately into the presence of the Lord. What is so interesting about this man and his conversion was that he was not able to go to church or be baptized or live one full day for the Lord, for he died on the cross that day. But he was forgiven. He believed and he was saved. He is now in paradise with the angels and patriarchs and prophets and apostles and martyrs and confessors and reformers and all the saints.

---

[4] For more on the biblical teaching on imputed righteousness, see John Piper, *Counted Righteous in Christ* (Wheaton, IL: Crossway, 2002).

[5] The request, "Remember me" in verse 42, is simply a way of asking for mercy. We see this, for instance, in Psalm 25.6-7.

He doesn't deserve to be there, but neither do you or I. Salvation is by grace alone received through faith alone.

Jesus taught salvation by faith alone. John 6.28-29 states, "Then they said to him, 'What must we do, to be doing the works of God?' Jesus answered them, 'This is the work of God, that you believe in him whom he has sent.'" Notice they asked him what were the "works" (plural) that they had to do to be right with God. Jesus responded by saying that the only "work" (singular) that was necessary was faith. He didn't give them a list of things to do; he simply told them to believe. That is what God requires for salvation. Paul taught the same thing. Here are a few examples.

- "For I am not ashamed of this Good News about Christ. It is the power of God at work, saving everyone who believes—the Jew first and also the Gentile. This Good News tells us how God makes us right in his sight. This is accomplished from start to finish by faith. As the Scriptures say, 'It is through faith that a righteous person has life'" (Rom 1.16-17 NLT).

- "For we hold that one is justified by faith apart from works of the law" (Rom 3.28).

- "We know that a person is not justified by works of the law but through faith in Jesus Christ, so we also have believed in Christ Jesus, in order to be justified by faith in Christ and not by works of the law, because by works of the law no one will be justified" (Gal 2.16).

- "For by grace you have been saved through faith. And this is not your own doing; it is the gift of God, not a result of works, so that no one may boast" (Eph 2.8-9).

Paul's testimony was one of salvation by faith alone. Here is his story in his own words. "If anyone else thinks he has reason for confidence in the flesh, I have more: circumcised on the eighth day, of the people of Israel, of the tribe of Benjamin, a Hebrew of Hebrews; as to the law, a Pharisee; as to zeal, a persecutor of the church; as to righteousness under the law, blameless. But whatever gain I had, I counted as loss for the sake of Christ. Indeed, I count everything as loss because of the surpassing worth of knowing Christ Jesus my Lord. For his sake I have suffered the loss of all things and count them as rubbish, in order that I may gain Christ and be found in him, not having a righteousness of my own that comes from the law, but that which comes through faith in Christ, the righteousness from God that depends on faith" (Phil 3.4-9). Paul was a very religious man with a very religious heritage, but he learned not to trust in these. His religious zeal and pedigree were "rubbish" compared to Christ. He laid aside his self-produced righteousness in order to receive by faith a God-given righteousness. If anyone could have been saved by works, it was Paul but he wasn't. He was saved by faith alone. That is the only way to be saved.[6]

Good Deeds

Salvation by faith alone does not mean that good deeds are unimportant or unnecessary. We are not saved because we do good, but we are saved in order to do good. Good deeds are not the cause but the result of salvation. Psalm 37.3 states, "Trust in the LORD, and do good." Doing good follows trusting in the Lord. Ephesians 2.10 reveals that good deeds are the result of receiving salvation as a free gift by faith. Good deeds are the evidence of saving faith. Martin Luther said we are saved by faith alone, but faith that is alone is not saving faith. True faith empowers us to live for the Lord. Galatians 5.6 says, "For in Christ Jesus neither circumcision nor uncircumcision has any value. The only thing that counts is faith expressing itself through

---

[6] For other verses that support *sola fide*, see Hab 2.4; Mark 5.36; John 3.16; 6.47; Acts 16.30-31; Rom 4.5; 5.1; 1 Cor 1.21; 1 John 5.4.

love" (NIV). Faith expresses itself and gives evidence of itself through acts of love.

Saving faith involves action. We haven't truly believed in Christ unless we act on this belief. Luther explained it this way, "Everything depends upon faith. The person who does not have faith is like someone who has to cross the sea, but is so frightened that he does not trust the ship. And so he stays where he is, and is never saved, because he will not get on board and cross over."[7] Faith gets on board. Faith believes that Jesus alone is Savior and that through him sin and death have been conquered. Therefore, a person who has saving faith is not afraid to die and is willing to give up his life for Christ, for he knows that an eternal inheritance awaits him in heaven. Faith in Christ and following Christ are inseparable.

This type of faith is a gift from God. I am not saying that God believes for us or makes us believe. I am simply saying that without God's grace and enablement we would never believe in Jesus Christ. I can't boast that I have believed in Jesus, for I wouldn't have done so without God's help. Acts 18.27 says, "When he arrived, he greatly helped those who through grace had believed." They believed in Christ "through grace." God's grace enabled them to believe, and thus saving faith is a gift from God. The father of the son with an unclean spirit cried out to Jesus, "I believe; help my unbelief!" (Mark 9.24). Only the Lord can help us overcome our unbelief. Other verses that teach that faith is a gift are Ephesians 2.8-9, Philippians 1.29, and 1 Timothy 1.14. This idea is also affirmed in our hymnody. D. W. Whittle, for instance, shares how faith is a gift from God in his beloved hymn.

I know not how this saving faith
To me He did impart,
Nor how believing in His Word
Wrought peace within my heart.

---

[7] This quote is cited in Alister E. McGrath, *Theology: The Basics*, 2nd ed. (Malden, MA: Blackwell Publishing, 2008), 11.

I know not how the Spirit moves,
Convincing men of sin,
Revealing Jesus through the Word,
Creating faith in Him.

But what if your faith is weak or small? The disciples struggled with this. Often Jesus would say to them, "O you of little faith" (Matt 6.30; 8.26; 14.31; 16.8). The good news is that it's not the *size* of our faith that matters most, but the *object* of our faith. If a pond has a light, thin covering of ice over it, it will not hold me up if I walk out on it no matter how much I believe. But if it is really thick ice, it will hold me up even if I'm afraid or have some doubts. Jesus Christ is the object of our faith. He is rock solid and utterly reliable. We can trust in him and build our life on him. He will never fail us, even when our faith is weak. Yet, he is also able to strengthen our faith. Through the promises of his word, answered prayers, and encouragement from fellow believers, our faith is nurtured and grows strong.

Repentance and Baptism

If faith is the means of salvation, where do repentance and baptism come in? Actually, these are interconnected. Let's look at repentance first. Repentance and faith are two sides of the same coin. You won't repent unless you believe, and you haven't believed unless you've truly repented of your sin. Jesus said, "Repent and believe in the gospel" (Mark 1.15). Repentance is not simply feeling sorry for your sin, but turning from it and renouncing it. Like faith, repentance is also a gift from God.

- "Turn us again, O LORD God of hosts, cause thy face to shine; and we shall be saved" (Ps 80.19 KJV, see also vv. 3, 7).[8]

- "Turn us, O God of our salvation, and cause thine anger toward us to cease" (Ps 85.4 KJV).

---

[8] Notice the psalmist is asking God to "turn" him from his sin back to the Lord. He realizes that he will not or cannot do so in his own power.

- "God exalted him at his right hand as Leader and Savior, to give repentance to Israel and forgiveness of sins" (Acts 5.31).

- "When they heard this, they were silenced. And they praised God, saying, 'Then God has given even to the Gentiles the repentance that leads to life'" (Acts 11.18 NRSV).

- "God may perhaps grant them repentance leading to a knowledge of the truth" (2 Tim 2.25).

God is the one who grants us the ability to turn from our sin. Sin's grip on us is too great for us to do this on our own. We need divine grace to repent. So, are we saved by faith alone? Yes, but the faith that saves is a repenting faith. True faith is always accompanied by repentance.

Baptism is also connected to faith, and repentance too for that matter (Acts 2.38). Baptism is an outward, tangible expression of our faith and repentance. The biblical order for those responding to the gospel is to believe and be baptized. It's interesting that this is always the order given. Baptism never precedes faith; it always follows it (Acts 8.12; 18.8; Eph 4.5; cf. Mark 16.16). That is because without faith baptism has no significance. As James Dunn writes, "Baptism gives expression to faith, but without faith baptism is meaningless, an empty symbol."[9] Baptism has no magical power to it. By itself it cannot save us. In Acts, baptism never stands alone. People are told to repent and be baptized (2.38) or to repent (3.19; 17.30) or to believe (16.31), but never simply to be baptized. The command to be baptized is always accompanied by the command to do something else first or along with it.[10] Baptism cannot stand alone. Baptism finds its significance and confirming power in connection with faith and repentance.

Though baptism itself does not wash away sins or bestow the gift of the Spirit, it is a picture of the gospel. When we are immersed in

---

[9] James D. G. Dunn, *Baptism in the Holy Spirit* (Philadelphia: Westminster Press, 1970), 97.

[10] Ibid.

water, we demonstrate that we have died with Christ and risen with him to live a new life (Rom 6.3-4). Baptism is important and a clear command of Scripture, but faith is what matters most in terms of our response. In his most detailed exposition of the gospel, the Letter to the Romans, Paul mentions baptism only in two verses, but the words "faith" and "believe" occur over 60 times. This is not to diminish baptism, but it is to highlight that we are saved by faith in Christ, not by our baptism. We can be saved without baptism, but we can't be saved without faith.[11]

---

[11] I think if a person can be baptized there is no excuse not to. In Acts, converts were baptized immediately. However, if a person cannot be baptized due to health reasons or location, God understands. Baptism adds to our assurance, but it doesn't remove our sin. For more on baptism, see Thomas R. Schreiner and Shawn D. Wright, *Believer's Baptism* (Nashville: B & H Academic, 2006).

CHAPTER FIVE

Justification and Sanctification

❧

When God saves us, he really saves us. He saves us from the penalty and power of sin. Salvation is not only having our sins forgiven, but having our life transformed. Luke 19.8-9 reads, "And Zacchaeus stood and said to the Lord, 'Behold, Lord, the half of my goods I give to the poor. And if I have defrauded anyone of anything, I restore it fourfold.' And Jesus said to him, 'Today salvation has come to this house, since he also is a son of Abraham.'" Zacchaeus was a notorious sinner, a chief tax collector, yet he was transformed by his encounter with Jesus. The result was salvation, which resulted in a generous heart and acts of restitution. As is clear from this passage, salvation addresses our past, but it also reshapes our present and future. If all God did was forgive us and not change us, then we would keep doing what we did before. We need forgiveness and transformation. That is what the Lord offers us in the gospel. We refer to these acts as justification and sanctification.[1]

---

[1] Sanctification is used at times in the New Testament to speak of our initial consecration to the Lord in salvation (1 Cor 1.2). This is called positional sanctification. But sanctification language is also used to refer to our spiritual

Before looking at each of these individually, it is helpful to distinguish the two. Now it's important to point out that those who are justified are also sanctified. You can't be one without the other (1 Cor 1.30; 6.11). As Calvin states, "Christ does not justify anyone without also making him holy. It is an inseparable bond...Those whom he justifies, he sanctifies."[2] But they are different works that address different needs that we have as sinners. Here are some differences between justification and sanctification.

- In justification, God *declares* us righteous. In sanctification, he *makes* us righteous.

- Justification address the *guilt* of sin, whereas sanctification addresses the *power* of sin.

- Justification is what God does *for* us. Sanctification is what God does *in* us.

- Our *status* is changed in justification. Our *nature* is changed in sanctification.

- In justification, the work is *complete* the moment it is received. In sanctification, the work is *progressive* and will not be complete in this life.

Justification

The doctrine of justification is not a side issue. It is fundamental to the gospel and our experience of the gospel in salvation. Therefore, it's imperative that we understand the meaning of justification. The following are some helpful definitions.

- John Calvin — "So we simply interpret justification as the acceptance with which God receives us into his favour as

---

transformation and growth (Rom 6.22; 1 Thess 4.3; 5.23; Heb 12.14; 1 Pet 1.15-16). It is in this latter sense that I am speaking of sanctification in this chapter. We may call this progressive or practical sanctification.

[2] Calvin, *The Institutes of Christian Religion*, 3.16.1.

if we were righteous: this justification consists in the forgiveness of sins and the imputation of Christ's righteousness."[3]

- Thomas Watson — "It is an act of God's free grace, whereby he pardons all our sins, and accepts us as righteous in his sight, only for the righteousness of Christ, imputed to us, and received by faith alone."[4]

- Matthew Henry — "Justification, in the gospel sense, is the free forgiveness of a sinner, accepting him as righteous through the righteousness of Christ received by faith."[5]

- James Buchanan — "By justification we mean—man's acceptance with God, or his being regarded and treated as righteous in His sight—as the object of His favour, and not of His wrath; of His blessing, and not of His curse."[6]

- Philip Eveson — "Justification is a legal pronouncement made by God in the present, prior to the day of judgment, declaring sinners to be not guilty and therefore to be acquitted, by pardoning all their sins and reckoning them to be righteous in his sight, on the basis of Christ, their representative and substitute, whose righteousness in life and death is put to their account when in self-despairing trust they look to him alone for salvation."[7]

---

[3] Ibid., 3.11.2.

[4] Thomas Watson, *A Body of Divinity* (Carlisle, PA: The Banner of Truth Trust, 2003), 226. This book was originally published in 1692, and this definition of justification is taken from the Westminster Shorter Catechism.

[5] This quote is found in his remarks on Titus 3.7 in his well-known commentary.

[6] James Buchanan, *The Doctrine of Justification* (Carlisle, PA: The Banner of Truth Trust, 1997), 17. This book was originally published in 1867 and is a classic on the subject of justification.

[7] Philip Eveson, *The Great Exchange* (Bromley, England: Day One Publications, 1996), 193. This is the most clear and complete definition of justification I have found.

- Brian Vickers — "Justification, foundational for salvation, is the legal declaration from God that a person stands before him forgiven and as one who lives up to the entirety of God's will."[8]

- Sam Storms — "Justification is God's legal declaration that the righteousness of his Son, Jesus Christ, has been imputed or reckoned to us so that we stand in his presence fully accepted and forgiven by faith alone."[9]

These are incisive, biblically sound definitions of justification. They are helpful, for we need an accurate, biblical understanding of justification; otherwise, we will lack the assurance of salvation and be hindered in our progress in sanctification. I would like to point out six characteristics of justification. It is forensic, instantaneous, complete, free, lasting, and essential. Let's look at each of these characteristics.

Justification is *forensic* in nature. This is why a few of the above definitions spoke of it as a "legal declaration." Justification is forensic language, language used in the court of law. Being justified is the opposite of being condemned (Prov 17.15; Rom 8.33-34). If you are condemned you are not justified, and if you are justified you will not be condemned. When we are justified, we are pronounced and accepted by God as fully forgiven and perfectly righteous in his sight. It is a legal declaration by God that effects a changed status before him—we go from being condemned sinners to being righteous sons and daughters. God treats us now as if we had never sinned. Some refer to this as legal fiction. But there is nothing fictional about it. Our sins are truly forgiven and our status before God has been truly changed. Because of what Christ has done on our behalf, God accepts us as perfectly righteous in his sight.

We see this in one of Paul's great statements on justification. He writes, "For our sake he made him to be sin who knew no sin, so that

---

[8] Brian Vickers, *Justification by Grace through Faith* (Phillipsburg, NJ: P & R Publishing, 2013), 2.

[9] Sam Storms, *Kept for Jesus* (Wheaton, IL: Crossway, 2015), 79.

in him we might become the righteousness of God" (2 Cor 5.21). What does it mean to become the righteousness of God? To understand this, it's necessary to look at the first half of this verse. In what way was Christ made sin for us? Of course, he was not actually a sinner. This verse says he knew no sin, that is, he committed no sin. He was made a sinner by God in the sense that he was treated as a sinner on the cross when he died in our place. In the same way, we become the righteousness of God not in that we are righteous ourselves, but in that God treats us, views us, and accepts us as perfectly righteous in his sight based on Christ's substitutionary death. Our sins are imputed to Christ, and his righteousness is imputed to us. God legally declares us righteous and acceptable before him because of the cross.

John Bunyan tells of his grand realization of this truth. He writes, "One day, as I was passing in the field, and that too with some dashes on my conscience, fearing lest yet all was not right, suddenly this sentence fell upon my soul, *Thy righteousness is in heaven*; and methought withal, I saw with the eyes of my soul Jesus Christ at God's right hand, there, I say, as my righteousness; so that wherever I was, or whatever I was doing, God could not say of me, *He wants [lacks] my righteousness*, for that was just before him. I also saw moreover, that it was not my good frame of heart that made my righteousness better, nor yet my bad frame that made my righteousness worse: for my righteousness was Jesus Christ himself, *the same yesterday, and today, and forever* (Heb. 13:8)...Now Christ was all; all my wisdom, all my righteousness, all my sanctification, and all my redemption."[10] The latter part of this quote is a reference to 1 Corinthians 1.30: "It is because of him that you are in Christ Jesus, who has become for us wisdom from God—that is, our righteousness, holiness and redemption" (NIV). If Jesus Christ is our righteousness, then we are perfectly justified, for his righteousness is perfect. Again, as Bunyan testifies, "I saw that I

---

[10] John Bunyan, *Grace Abounding to the Chief of Sinners* (New York: Penguin Books, 1987), 59-60. This classic was originally published in 1666.

needed a perfect righteousness to present me without fault before God and that this righteousness was nowhere to be found but in the person of Jesus Christ."[11]

Justification is *instantaneous*. When we believe in Christ, we are instantly justified by God and before God. We are not put on a probationary standing before the Lord. We do not have to prove ourselves first before he pronounces us as just and holy in his sight. He accepts us immediately. When the prodigal son returned, he was immediately given the best robe[12] to put on, a ring to wear, sandals for his feet, and a feast to celebrate his return (Luke 15.22-24). His father instantly accepted him and reinstated him as his son. God does the same for us. One moment we are condemned before the Lord; the next moment we are righteous in his sight. This is the miracle and blessing of justification.

Justification is *complete*. Watson explains, "Though there are degrees in grace, yet not in justification; one is not justified more than another; the weakest believer is as perfectly justified as the strongest."[13] We grow in sanctification, but not in justification. We are either 100% justified or not justified at all. Romans 8.1 says, "There is therefore now no condemnation for those who are in Christ Jesus." For those who are united to Christ Jesus by faith, there is "no condemnation"—none at all. Colossians 2.13 states, "He forgave us all our sins" (NIV). With all our sins forgiven, our justified standing before the Lord is complete. And it is complete right now. Paul says that there is "now" no condemnation.

Though the final verdict will not be pronounced publicly until the last day, we are already assured of that verdict and live in its joy right now. As he approached the prospect of death, Paul wrote, "From now on there is reserved for me the crown of righteousness, which the Lord, the righteous judge, will give me on that day, and

---

[11] Ibid., 24.

[12] The reference to the best robe reminds me of the robe of righteousness that only God can give us (Isa 61.10).

[13] Watson, *A Body of Divinity*, 228-29.

not only to me but also to all who have longed for his appearing" (2 Tim 4.8 NRSV). Notice that this righteousness is *God-given* ("will give me"), *forensic* ("the righteous judge"), *perfect* ("the crown of righteousness"), *certain* ("there is reserved for me"), *available* ("but also to all"), and *future* in its public pronouncement ("on that day"). We are fully justified in the present moment, and thus we know what the verdict will be on that day. Without this reality and the knowledge of it, we could have no assurance of salvation. But with it, we can look forward to the return of Christ with eager anticipation.

Justification is *free*. We cannot earn or merit a right standing before the Lord. We are justified by grace (Rom 3.24; Tit 3.7). Grace is God's unmerited favor and kindness shown to hell-deserving sinners. Grace is the reason we are justified. Why would God send his Son to die for our sins? Why would God accept that sacrifice on our behalf? Grace is the reason. We are saved by grace from beginning to end, and that includes our justification. It is a free gift received by faith alone. Romans 4.5 teaches that God "justifies the ungodly." How can this be? God justifies the ungodly because Christ died for the ungodly (Rom 5.6). Because of the price that Jesus paid, we can receive "the gift of righteousness" (Rom 5.17). Justification is a free gift based on the costly death of God's Son.

Justification is *lasting*. It is not based on our feelings or perfect performance. It does not wax and wane. We are not justified in the morning, then non-justified in the afternoon, then re-justified again in the evening. We are justified period. John 5.24 states, "Truly, truly, I say to you, whoever hears my word and believes him who sent me has eternal life. He does not come into judgment, but has passed from death to life." We will not come into judgment because we have already "passed from death to life." The forgiveness we have from the Lord is full, free, and final. No accusation can stand against us. No one can condemn us, for Christ has died for us and is interceding for us at the Father's right hand (Rom 8.33-34).

Justification is *essential*. There is no salvation without justification. Some have wrongly made justification the sum and substance of the gospel in its entirety, or at least close to it. There is more to the gospel than justification, but certainly not less. Vickers helpfully explains, "Justification by faith is not the whole of the gospel, but there is no gospel without justification by faith."[14] Watson states, "Justification is the very hinge and pillar of Christianity. An error about justification is dangerous, like a defect in a foundation."[15] Justification is essential because we are justified by the blood of Christ (Rom 5.9). The blood is the basis of our justification. Good works, the law, religion, our own efforts—none of these could ever serve as the basis of our acceptance with God. The atoning blood of Christ is the only foundation for a right standing with God. The blood satisfies God's justice and covers all our sins. We can stand before our holy God without fear because of the blood. Without this justified standing before the Lord based on the blood, there is no hope and no salvation (Ps 130.3-4; 143.2). Justification is absolutely essential. There is no eternal life without it.

It may be helpful to point out the various prepositional phrases connected with justification, all which are found in Romans. We are justified by grace (3.24), by faith (5.1), by the blood (5.9), and by God (8.33). Grace is the cause of justification, faith is the means of receiving it, the blood of Christ is its basis, and God is the author of justification. Ultimately, God is the one who justifies us, but he does so because of his grace and based on the death of his Son, and it is received by us through faith. Faith in Christ is the means by which we receive our justified status before God. We are not declared righteous through the law or our good works, but through faith. Faith is not meritorious itself, but is simply the means of justification—it is the outreached hand that receives God's free gift.

James and Jesus

But what about James? Did he not contradict or challenge what Paul said about justification by faith alone? He wrote, "You see that a person is justified by works and not by faith alone" (Jam 2.24).

---

[14] Vickers, *Justification by Grace through Faith*, 2-3.

[15] Watson, *A Body of Divinity*, 226.

The context makes clear that James is not saying that our works merit justification, but that saving faith is more than intellectual faith: it is a faith that results in good works. Paul would agree (Gal 5.6). These apostles were addressing different situations. Paul was writing to those who were adding legalistic stipulations to the gospel, and his response was that we're saved by faith in Christ alone. James was writing to those who believed in God but were not living out their faith in a practical manner. His response was to remind them that mere intellectual faith is insufficient to save. Paul and James would both agree that faith always produces good works. I think both would also agree that good works are not the cause of salvation, for one of James's examples of justification is Rahab the prostitute (Jam 2.25).

Speaking of Paul and justification, some think that this teaching was unique to him. Certainly he emphasized it more than any other New Testament author. However, this teaching is also found in Acts 13.38-39. Plus, Jesus himself taught justification by faith alone. We see this in the Parable of the Pharisee and the Tax Collector (Luke 18.9-14). Two men went to the temple to pray. One was a Pharisee who was very religious yet self-righteous and judgmental. The other was a tax collector who was sinful and despised by his fellow Jews for his greed, dishonesty, and collaboration with the Roman Empire. In his prayer the tax collector could only say, "God, be merciful to me, a sinner!" He had no righteousness in which to trust or plead. All he could do was acknowledge his sin and ask for God's mercy. And that was enough! Verse 14 reads, "I tell you, this man went down to his house justified, rather than the other. For everyone who exalts himself will be humbled, but the one who humbles himself will be exalted." The tax collector was instantly and fully justified by God in response to his faith.

Sanctification

Let's now look at sanctification. Sanctification is a big word, but it's also a biblical word. It is synonymous with the word holiness. In the Old Testament, the Hebrew word *qadash* ("to set apart as holy, sanctify") and its cognates are used over 640 times. Anyone who believes in the Bible believes in sanctification. Yet, many are confused about what it means to be sanctified. Let me attempt to make its meaning clear. To be sanctified means to be set apart by God for his purpose. It means that we belong exclusively to God. When we are sanctified, we no longer belong to the world or to ourselves; we belong to the Lord. We are his, and thus we are to be like him and to do his will.

Sanctification is not the basis of our acceptance with God. This is essential to understand from the beginning; otherwise, we will lack assurance and peace in our walk with God. Living a sanctified life is the will of God for every believer (1 Thess 4.3), but our sanctification is not what makes us right with God or acceptable in his sight. We are "justified by his blood" (Rom 5.9), which means it is the blood of Christ that renders us righteous and acceptable in God's holy presence. The hymn writer affirms, "This is all my hope and peace, nothing but the blood of Jesus. This is all my righteousness, nothing but the blood of Jesus." As we have seen, to be justified is to be pronounced and accepted as perfectly righteous in God's sight. Justification deals with our standing before God. In Christ we stand before God guiltless, free from all condemnation (Rom 8.1, 33-34). Sanctification, in contrast, deals with our character and lifestyle. These two works or blessings are not the same.

Without a clear understanding of justification and its distinction from sanctification, we will lack the assurance of salvation, or worse, fall into a works-based righteousness. We will think that God accepts us or loves us because we are holy. We may even begin to expand what holiness means beyond Scripture itself. This is the temptation of legalism. Legalism is the attempt to earn God's favor either by our good works or by adding our own list of do's and don'ts to God's commands. But sanctification is not about human rules or traditions. It's about God's holy character being formed in us by his Spirit.

Legalism is usually accompanied by guilt—false guilt. There is guilt and then there is false guilt. False guilt is when we feel bad or condemned even though we haven't done anything wrong in God's sight. False guilt is harmful. It can lead to depression and actually drive us away from God and his love. Here are some causes of false guilt: an overly sensitive conscience,[16] Satan's accusations, trying to live up to the expectations of other people, and the influence of a legalistic church. It may be helpful in this context to distinguish between conviction and condemnation.

- Conviction reveals our *sin*. Condemnation reveals our *legalistic hang-ups*.

- Conviction is very *specific*. Condemnation is *vague* and *hazy*.

- Conviction is *needed* at times. Condemnation is *never good*.

- Conviction leads to *transformation*. Condemnation leads to *desperation*.

- Conviction is from the *Holy Spirit*. Condemnation is from the *devil*.

Sanctification is never perfect in this life. In the Lord's Prayer, Jesus taught his followers to pray for forgiveness (Matt 6.12; Luke 11.4). This is not a prayer of salvation; it is a prayer for a disciple to pray. Jesus knew we would need this prayer because of our imperfection, and it shows that God is willing to forgive us when we sin. We are also told to forgive the wrongs committed against us by

---

[16] Wesley provides prudent advice on this subject: "But sometimes this excellent quality, tenderness of conscience, is carried to an extreme. We find some who fear where no fear is; who are continually condemning themselves without cause; imagining some things to be sinful, which the Scripture nowhere condemns; and supposing other things to be their duty, which the Scripture nowhere enjoins. This is properly termed a scrupulous conscience, and is a sore evil. It is highly expedient to yield to it as little as possible; rather it is a matter of earnest prayer, that you may be delivered from this sore evil, and may recover a sound mind; to which nothing would contribute more, than the converse of a pious and judicious friend" ("On Conscience" in *The Works of John Wesley*, 3rd ed. [Peabody, MA: Hendrickson Publishers, 1991], 7.191).

fellow believers in the church (Col 3.13). Here we see that Christians are not perfectly sanctified and can disappoint or wound us at times. We are even admonished to confess our sins to one another (Jam 5.16). These commands—to pray, to forgive, and to confess—clearly reveal that God's people, though converted and no longer under the dominion of sin (Rom 6.14), are still imperfect and in need of God's grace. Sanctification is never complete in this life.

But what about "entire sanctification"? The Bible does talk about being sanctified or holy in every area of our life. For instance, 1 Peter 1.15 states, "Be holy in all your conduct." Also, 2 Corinthians 7.1 says, "Since we have these promises, beloved, let us cleanse ourselves from every defilement of body and spirit, bring holiness to completion in the fear of God." As you can see, sanctification is to be entire or thorough, impacting our inward and outward life, our will, our thoughts, our motivations, our conduct, our time, our everything. There is no area of our life that is to be hidden from God's sanctifying influence. However, this does not mean that we are perfect in this life (Phil 3.12-14). Though sanctification touches every area of our life, it is not perfect in any of these areas. Who can say, for instance, that they cannot be more sanctified in terms of their thoughts or motivation? Second Peter 3.18 admonishes us to "grow in the grace and knowledge of our Lord and Savior Jesus Christ."

Sanctification is a lifelong process. We should be growing in our faith and obedience until the day we die. Some practical means to help us grow are as follows.

- Reading the Bible — Just as we need food to survive and grow, so we need God's word to grow spiritually as believers. The Bible teaches us who God is, what he expects from us, and what he has promised to do for us. We should read from the Bible every day.[17]

---

[17] For help in reading and understanding the Bible, see Gordon D. Fee and Douglas Stuart, *How to Read the Bible for All Its Worth*, 4th ed. (Grand Rapids, MI: Zondervan, 2014).

- Praying — No relationship can thrive without regular communication. Prayer is simply communicating with God. Through prayer we receive strength and guidance to do his will.

- Being involved in a Christ-centered church — We were never meant to live the Christian life alone. That's why God gave us the church. Our brothers and sisters in Christ encourage us, pray for us, and hold us accountable.[18]

- Receiving the Lord's Supper — The Lord's Supper is not a saving act, but it is a means of grace. When received in faith, it is a means of sanctifying grace through the work of the Holy Spirit in our life.

- Confessing our sins to one another — James 5.16 states, "Confess your sins to one another and pray for another, that you may be healed." I think we neglect this spiritual discipline way too often. Ultimately, we confess our sins to God, for only he can forgive them. But there are times when we should confess our transgressions to a trusted friend as well. When we do, we can receive prayer support, encouragement, and guidance in how to overcome in the future.

- Ministering to people in need — We grow as we serve others and use the grace and gifts God has given to us. A profession of faith is not enough; we need to put our faith into action. And when we do, we will grow.

These are means of grace to help us grow, and we will be growing our whole Christian life. Sanctification is never finished in this life. If sanctification were perfect in this life, then there would be

---

[18] For a great book on the church, see Edmund P. Clowney, *The Church* (Downers Grove, IL: InterVarsity, 1995).

little or no need for glorification. And just as we need to distinguish between justification and sanctification, so we need to do the same with sanctification and glorification. Glorification is when we will be glorified and fully transformed into the image of Christ at his return. First John 3.2 explains, "Beloved, we are God's children now, and what we will be has not yet appeared; but we know that when he appears we shall be like him, because we shall see him as he is." Whatever remains unlike Christ will be instantly and miraculously transformed into his likeness when he returns. This is the hope and beauty of glorification. This is no excuse to stop growing, for this verse is followed by the statement: "Everyone who thus hopes in him purifies himself as he is pure" (v. 3). "Purify" is in the present tense in the Greek, which speaks of an ongoing purification. As we progress in our walk with God and anticipate Christ's return, we are to keep growing in a pure, sanctified life.

Sanctification is the work of God. It is both the will of God and the work of God. A famous text on sanctification states, "May God himself, the God of peace, sanctify you through and through. May your whole spirit, soul and body be kept blameless at the coming of our Lord Jesus Christ. The one who calls you is faithful, and he will do it" (1 Thess 5.23-24 NIV). It is the God of peace himself who sanctifies us, and he will be faithful to do it. We cannot sanctify ourselves. We can change this or that about ourselves outwardly, but we can't address our heart. Only God can create in us a clean heart. David prayed, "Create in me a clean heart, O God, and renew a right spirit within me" (Ps 51.10). The Hebrew word for "create" is *bara*, and in the Old Testament the subject of this word is always God. God is the only one who creates; he alone is Creator. And just as God created this world out of nothing (Gen 1.1), so he is able to create in us a clean heart no matter how dark or dirty our heart has become. He is able to do this through the power of his Holy Spirit. This Spirit is received at conversion (John 3.5; Rom 8.9), but we are to be filled with the Spirit too, and not just once but repeatedly (Acts 2.4; 4.31; Eph 5.18). There is no sanctification without the life-transforming power of the Holy Spirit.

Sanctification is not a dreary subject, but a joyful teaching and experience. Sanctification and wholeness go together. Where we are sanctified, we are whole and healthy. Living a sanctified life is not the same as living a bizarre, fanatical, or legalistic life; rather, it is a sane and healthy life lived for God's glory. It is being healthy in every area of our life—spiritually, mentally, emotionally, physically, and relationally. Sanctification and community go together. The desert fathers failed to grasp this point in Scripture, and the result was that they flocked to the desert in isolation to seek holiness. But we need each other. Whitefield once pointed out that if God said of Adam in paradise that it was not good for him to be alone, how much more is it not good for us to be alone in this world of sin! That's why God gave us the church. In the New Testament, the word "saint" is always used in the plural. The only exception is Philippians 4.21, where the communal emphasis is still found. We cannot be saints in isolation. We need each other. Yes, sanctification is the work of God, but he works through others to make us into the people he wants us to be.

CHAPTER SIX

The Assurance
of Salvation

☙❦❧

It's one thing to be saved; it's another thing to *know* that we're saved. God not only wants to save us. He also wants us to be assured of our salvation. He is a good Father, and thus he doesn't want us to live with unnecessary doubts in a state of spiritual confusion. He wants us to be filled with the joy of knowing that we belong to him and that he belongs to us.

A Scriptural Teaching

Jesus taught the assurance of salvation. He sent his disciples out to preach the gospel and cast out demons. They were very successful in their mission. But he warned them not to rejoice in ministerial success alone. Their chief joy was to be in Christ and his gift of eternal life. He said, "Do not rejoice in this, that the spirits are subject to you, but rejoice that your names are written in heaven" (Luke 10.20). We can't rejoice that our names are written in heaven, though, unless we *know* they are written there. This verse, therefore, assumes we can know we are saved and on our way to heaven. Paul also spoke of people whose names were in the book of life (Phil 4.3), which also assumes that he knew or believed they were saved. It's important also to point out that Jesus's words show that the joy of salvation is directly connected to the assurance of salvation. We cannot rejoice unless we know our names are written in heaven. Without this assurance we have no true and lasting joy.

Paul believed in the assurance of salvation. He writes, "The Spirit himself bears witness with our spirit that we are children of God" (Rom 8.16). It is the "Spirit himself" who provides us with assurance: the emphasis in this verse is on the role of the Spirit.[1] As Douglas Moo states, "The Holy Spirit is not only instrumental in making us God's children; he also makes us aware that we are God's children."[2] This verse in Romans can be understood either to mean that the Spirit testifies *with* our spirit or *to* our spirit. If it is the former, then there are two witnesses: our spirit and the Holy Spirit (cf. Deut 19.15). If it is the latter, then the focus is on the Spirit's direct confirmation to our spirit that we belong to God. The Spirit provides this confirmation by enabling us to pray, "Abba! Father!" (Rom 8.15). This prayer from a believing heart is the Spirit's way of testifying to our spirit that we are God's children.

So, does the Holy Spirit testify with our spirit or to it? It is possible that both are true. The Spirit testifies to our spirit, and thus our spirit then joins with the Spirit in acknowledging that we are God's children.[3] Whichever way we translate this verse, the result is the same in the sense that the Holy Spirit provides us with inner assurance that we are God's children. Paul's sense of assurance was so strong that later in this chapter he declared that nothing in all creation can separate us from God's love. He exclaims, "And I am convinced that nothing can ever separate us from God's love. Neither death nor life, neither angels nor demons, neither our fears for today

---

[1] Leon Morris, *The Epistle to the Romans* (Grand Rapids, MI: Eerdmans, 1988), 316.

[2] Douglas Moo, *The Epistle to the Romans* (Grand Rapids, MI: Eerdmans 1996), 503.

[3] Robert H. Mounce, *Romans* (Nashville: Broadman & Holman Publishers, 1995), 183 n. 163.

nor our worries about tomorrow—not even the powers of hell can separate us from God's love. No power in the sky above or in the earth below—indeed, nothing in all creation will ever be able to separate us from the love of God that is revealed in Christ Jesus our Lord" (Rom 8.38-39 NLT).

First John is a key book in the New Testament when it comes to the assurance of salvation. The Apostle John wrote this letter to help people know whether or not they were truly saved. He writes, "And this is the testimony, that God gave us eternal life, and this life is in his Son. Whoever has the Son has life; whoever does not have the Son of God does not have life. I write these things to you who believe in the name of the Son of God, that you may know that you have eternal life" (1 John 5.11-13). These verses show that John believed that we can "know" that we have eternal life. Therefore, he clearly teaches the assurance of salvation, and evidently he believed that this experience was both possible and normal. He speaks of eternal life as a gift already given to us by God. This gift is inseparably connected to his Son, Jesus Christ. John makes a simple connection: if we have the Son of God, then we have eternal life; if we don't have the Son of God, then we don't have eternal life. It's that simple. Like Paul, John also connected the assurance of salvation to the inner work of the Holy Spirit.[4] As 1 John 3.24 states, "And this is how we know that he lives in us: We know it by the Spirit he gave us" (NIV). Through the Spirit of God we are assured of our salvation.

New Testament Christianity would not make sense without the assurance of salvation. For example, the doctrine of justification assumes the assurance of salvation. Paul teaches that we are justified by faith and that we enjoy right now this status of being right with God. He writes, "Therefore, since we have been justified by faith, we have peace with God through our Lord Jesus Christ. Through him we have also obtained access by faith into this grace in which we stand, and we rejoice in hope of the glory of God" (Rom 5.1-2). As

---

[4] Dunn states, "It is important to realize that for Paul (and John) one of the highest and best works of the Spirit is the assurance of salvation" (*Baptism in the Holy Spirit*, 132).

we have seen, to be justified is to be treated and accepted as perfectly righteous in God's sight. This standing before God is not based on our merits or works; it is based on Christ's sacrificial death for us (Rom 3.24-25; 5.9). On the day of judgment we will be officially and publicly pronounced righteous and free from guilt in God's sight, but even now we enjoy this status of being justified and are assured what the final verdict will then be. As Romans 8.1 states, "Therefore, there is now no condemnation for those in Christ Jesus." Though we are convicted by the Spirit when we fall short, the threat of God's condemnation against us has been lifted. There is "now" no condemnation—none at all. We can know this and thus enjoy the assurance of our salvation.

Not only does justification assume the assurance of salvation, but so does adoption. Salvation is described as being adopted into God's family (Gal 4.4-7). One of the joys of adoption is knowing that we are children of God. Would God adopt us into his family without assuring us of this reality? That makes no sense. We want our children to take comfort in knowing that they belong to us and that we love them. God the Father is the same way. Through Christ he adopted us into his family and we now belong to him. He assures us of this reality (Rom 8.16). Adoption is a powerful indicator of God's love for us. A couple can have biological children by accident, but they cannot adopt by accident. Adoption requires forethought, planning, and choice. God chose us to be part of his family. He wants us, and he wants us to know that he wants us.

Objections to the Assurance of Salvation

There are those who think it's impossible to have the assurance of salvation in this life, believing instead that we just do the best we can and hope in the end that God will accept us. There are others who think the idea of assurance is too subjective. Who knows if it is the Holy Spirit who is assuring us of our salvation? Maybe it is just our emotions, or even worse, the evil one masquerading as an angel of light (2 Cor 11.14). Some would say it is presumptuous to testify to the assurance of salvation. To them only the proud would claim to know that they are saved, since no one knows for sure except God.

This may sound humble, but it fails to consider the very nature of salvation. The Bible is clear that one of the Spirit's tasks is to give us inward assurance of being saved. Of course, it is important to point out that the witness of the Spirit and the outward demonstration of a saved life go together. The former will not be present without the latter. Yet, a transformed life itself is not the cause of salvation, but the result. If salvation were based on our own good works and effort, then it would be subjective and presumptuous to claim the assurance of salvation here and now. But salvation is a free gift: we are saved by grace, not by works (Rom 6.23; Eph 2.8-9). Thus, we are not being prideful or overconfident when we rejoice that we are saved. We are giving all glory to God. Jesus told us to rejoice that our names are written in heaven. He wants us to enjoy this assurance.

Without this assurance we will be ineffective witnesses for Christ. How are we going to share salvation with others if we are not certain of our own salvation? If you were a salesperson, it would be difficult for you to sell a product that you doubted yourself or had no experience with. When we witness, we testify to something we know first-handedly. That's what a witness is. We don't have to know the entire Bible to be witnesses. We simply need to know Christ and tell how he changed our life. Those who are forgiven and transformed, and know that they are—they are the ones who are powerful witnesses for Christ (Mark 5.19; Luke 7.47). In fact, they alone are powerful witnesses.

Why Some Doubt Their Salvation

I had doubts about my salvation for a number of years after I was converted. In a way, I knew I was saved, but I lacked a settled confidence and peace that should have been mine as a Christian. I kept wondering, "Am I really ready to meet the Lord? Is my life what it ought to be?" I think a lot of Christians struggle with the assurance of salvation. Here are some reasons why I think this is true.

First, they begin to look to their performance rather than to Christ alone. After being saved they subtly shift their focus from Christ and his saving grace to their own godliness. They ask themselves, "Have I prayed enough? Have I given enough? Do I read the Bible often enough? Am I worthy to go to heaven?" Yet, our focus should not be on ourselves. We should make sure that we have the fruit of salvation, but our focus should be on Christ and his all-sufficient, atoning sacrifice for our sin.

Gilbert Stafford shares the struggles he had with the assurance of salvation and how they were connected with being too worried about his performance rather than focusing on Christ alone. He explains, "During one period of my college years, I was excessively worried about the security of my salvation. I made continual use of the prayer room on the third floor of Anderson College's 'Old Main.' Several times a day I would go to that small room and seek assurance of my salvation. Each time I would pray through and then leave with a sense of security. However, before long I would again feel convicted about a fleeting thought, an attitude, or an action. Immediately I would feel that I had lost my salvation and would return to the prayer room to be converted all over again.

"I was in spiritual and emotional turmoil because I was operating on the wrong assumption that the security of my salvation rested in the perfection of my thought processes, emotional urges, and deeds. I was in bondage and needed release.

"What a glorious discovery it was to learn that the security of my salvation rests in the perfection of God's work in Christ and in his keeping power, and that what God requires of us is to stay in the yes-position of faith. In the course of time I learned to trust in him and to abide in him, knowing that as I did my salvation was absolutely secure. I learned that I was not cast out of the saving life of Christ every time my thought processes were not perfect, or every time my emotional urges were troublesome, or every time my actions left something to be desired. Of course, the Holy Spirit continued convicting me of that which was not pleasing to God, and when he did I repented and experienced his forgiveness. That meant that I was learning how to live the life of salvation. Instead of feeling cast out each time I was convicted, I knew that I was abiding securely within the life of him who was my perfect redemption. From that time forward I have had a sense of confidence in the perfect work of Christ. I no longer trust in *me* but in *him*."[5]

We are not perfect ourselves, but we trust in the perfect sacrifice of Christ and one day we will be perfect in heaven. One of my favorite devotionals is *Morning by Morning* by Spurgeon. In the June 28th reading, he explains what I am emphasizing here about focusing on Christ. He writes, "Remember, therefore, it is not your hold of Christ that saves you—it is Christ; it is not your joy in Christ that saves you—it is Christ; it is not even faith in Christ, though that be the instrument—it is Christ's blood and merits; therefore, look not so much to your hand with which you are grasping Christ, as to Christ; look not to your hope, but to Jesus, the source of your hope; look not to your faith, but to Jesus, the author and finisher of your faith."

Second, some question their salvation because they depend too much on their feelings. If they feel saved, then they believe they are saved; but if they don't feel saved, then they think they are lost. This is a horrible way to live. Our feelings are probably the least reliable part about us. We are saved by faith, not by feelings. We are to trust in God's promises rather than in our emotions. P. T. Forsyth said, "Our faith is not in our experience, but in our Savior." There is a poem attributed to Martin Luther that sums this up well.

Feelings come and feelings go,
And feelings are deceiving.
My warrant is the word of God;
Naught else is worth believing.

---

[5] Gilbert W. Stafford, *The Life of Salvation* (Anderson, IN: Warner Press, 1979), 87-88. In the next chapter, we will see that it is God by his grace who enables us to stay in this "yes-position of faith."

Though all my heart should feel condemned
At want of some sweet token,
There is one greater than my heart
Whose word cannot be broken.

I'll trust in God's unchanging word
Till soul and body sever;
For though all things shall pass away,
His word shall stand forever.

Third, some doubt their salvation because they think their conversion experience must be like someone else's. There are things that must be true of every conversion experience such as a sincere faith in Christ. But other aspects are not essential. We should not expect our conversion experience to be like someone else's. Maybe our conversion was not as dramatic or spectacular as the conversion of Saul of Tarsus, for instance. But that is not what's important. What matters is that we trusted in Christ and he saved us. It may also be helpful to point out that our experience of assurance is unique as well. Some are more prone to doubt than others, and it takes more to provide them with reassurance. Also, some walk closer to God than others. Charles Brown explains, "It must be remembered that these spiritual privileges are enjoyed in different degrees by every Christian. That is to say, the witness of the Spirit is the same to all just as the sun is the same to all, but as some people have better eyesight to benefit by the light of the sun, so some Christians are more spiritual and thus better able to appropriate these privileges of the assurance of salvation. It would be a pity if this doctrine, meant to sustain and comfort the hearts of the saints, should be misinterpreted so as to become a burden instead of a consolation."[6]

Last, some are simply under Satan's attack. He's called "the accuser of our brethren" for a reason (Rev 12.10 NKJV). Satan

---

[6] Charles E. Brown, *The Meaning of Salvation* (Anderson, IN: Gospel Trumpet, 1950; reprint, Salem, OH: Schmul Publishing, 1982), 132.

attacks us at times and tries to get us to doubt our salvation. He even tried to get Jesus to doubt his sonship. He said to Jesus in the wilderness, "*If* you are the Son of God, command these stones to become loaves of bread" (Matt 4.3, italics added). He tried to put doubt in Jesus's mind and tempted him to prove his sonship by performing a miracle that was focused on self rather than on ministry to others. Jesus wisely resisted. Satan attacks us as well. He reminds us of all our past and present sins and shortcomings, and he tells us that God doesn't love us or want us any longer. This, however, is simply not true. Satan cannot separate us from God's love. If we take up the shield of faith and resist him, he must flee. We are saved and Christ lives in us; therefore, we can defeat Satan and live with the joyful assurance of salvation.

- "In addition to all this, take up the shield of faith, with which you can extinguish all the flaming arrows of the evil one" (Eph 6.16 NIV).

- "God made you alive with Christ, for he forgave all our sins. He canceled the record of the charges against us and took it away by nailing it to the cross. In this way, he disarmed the spiritual rulers and authorities. He shamed them publicly by his victory over them on the cross" (Col 2.13-15 NLT).

- "Submit yourselves therefore to God. Resist the devil, and he will flee from you" (Jam 4.7).

- "Greater is he that is in you, than he that is in the world" (1 John 4.4 KJV).

- "And I heard a loud voice in heaven, saying, 'Now the salvation and the power and the kingdom of our God and the authority of his Christ have come, for the accuser of our brothers has been thrown down, who accuses them day and night before our God. And they have conquered him by the blood of the Lamb and by the word of their

testimony, for they loved not their lives even unto death'"
(Rev 12.10-11).

Hope and the Assurance of Salvation

Hope in the New Testament speaks of confident expectation. It involves certainty rather than anxiety or doubt. To say you hope that something will happen, therefore, means that you believe it will happen, you are sure it will. Consequently, when hope is used in connection with salvation and eternal life, it speaks of the assurance of salvation. It speaks of being sure, not only of our present salvation, but of salvation in the life to come. It speaks of a settled, confident assurance that God has prepared heaven for us and therefore will watch over and protect us until we reach our heavenly destination. We see this in how hope in the following verses is used in connection with our future state or experience in heaven.

"For through the Spirit, by faith, we ourselves eagerly wait for *the hope of righteousness*" (Gal 5.5, italics added). The hope of righteousness is the assurance that we will be publicly declared as righteous in God's presence on the last day. We are justified already by faith (Rom 5.1). Hence, we know now what the final, public verdict will be. God is the one who has justified us, so no one can condemn us (Rom 8.33-34). We will be welcomed into heaven as God's righteous children clothed with the merits of Christ himself. "When He shall come with trumpet sound, O may I then in Him be found, dressed in His righteousness alone, faultless to stand before the throne. On Christ, the solid Rock, I stand; all other ground is sinking sand."

"To them God chose to make known how great among the Gentiles are the riches of the glory of this mystery, which is Christ in you, *the hope of glory*" (Col 1.27, italics added). The hope of glory refers to the assurance that we will be glorified and share in the glory of God. God's glory will be revealed and experienced in a full, direct, ever-conscious way in heaven. Romans 8.30 states, "And those whom he predestined he also called, and those whom he called he also justified, and those whom he justified he also glorified."

Notice that "glorified" is in the past tense. We are assured now of glorification then.

"But since we belong to the day, let us be sober, having put on the breastplate of faith and love, and for a helmet *the hope of salvation*" (1 Thess 5.8, italics added). The hope of salvation is the hope of final salvation. Salvation in the New Testament is past, present, and future. We have been saved (justification and regeneration), we are being saved (sanctification), and we will be saved (glorification). To speak of the hope of salvation for believers refers to future salvation, namely, salvation from God's wrath on the day of judgment (1 Thess 1.10; 5.9-10). We need not fear the day of judgment then as believers. For us it is "the day of redemption" (Eph 4.30). It is a day we look forward to, not one we fear or dread.

"So that being justified by his grace we might become heirs according to *the hope of eternal life*" (Tit 3.7, italics added). The hope of eternal life is the assurance that we will live forever with Christ. Eternal life is not just unending life, but unending life in fellowship with God and in a state of unending, ever-increasing enjoyment of God. In a sense, we already have eternal life. "I write these things to you who believe in the name of the Son of God, that you may know that you have eternal life" (1 John 5.13). God wants us to know this. He wants us to be assured of present salvation as well as salvation in the world to come. He wants us to live the Christian life with joy, assurance, and hope. Eternal life is ours now and will be ours forevermore. This is our hope. This is our joy. This is our confidence. This is also one of the reasons we give God all the glory for our salvation. He has saved us, he is saving us, and he will save us. "Behold, God is my salvation" (Isa 12.2). He is our salvation from beginning to end.

CHAPTER SEVEN

Kept by the Power of God

❦

As I've mentioned at different points, salvation is past, present, and future. Salvation is not just having our sins forgiven and being progressively transformed in this life; it is receiving our eternal inheritance and spending eternity with the Lord. God is faithful in all three aspects of salvation: he is faithful to pardon, purify, and preserve us. As Spurgeon explains, "True religion is supernatural at its beginning, supernatural in its continuance, and supernatural in its close. It is the work of God from first to last." That is to say, what God begins, he finishes. First Peter 1.3-5 states, "Blessed be the God and Father of our Lord Jesus Christ! According to his great mercy, he has caused us to be born again to a living hope through the resurrection of Jesus Christ from the dead, to an inheritance that is imperishable, undefiled, and unfading, kept in heaven for you, who by God's power are being guarded through faith for a salvation ready to be revealed in the last time." God preserves the inheritance for us and preserves us for the inheritance.

This passage says we are kept or guarded by God's power. The phrase, "by God's power," comes first in the Greek in verse 5 for emphasis. We are weak, frail, and susceptible to temptation, but God in his almighty power can keep us safe to the end. Scripture also emphasizes how we are preserved by God's faithfulness (1 Cor 1.8-9) and his love (Rom 8.38-39). Why does God preserve us? Because he is faithful and loving. How does he preserve us? By his great power active in our lives. This reminds me of a story I read about an elderly Scottish minister who visited a godly lady who was dying. He said to her, "What if at the last the Lord were to desert you?" She responded, "That would never happen. You see, if he did, he would lose far more than I." "How is that?" he asked. She quietly but confidently replied, "Well, I might lose my soul, but he would lose his honor and that would never happen."[1] God's honor is at stake in preserving his people to the end. There is no honor in starting a work and then leaving it incomplete. Thus, God finishes what he starts. "And I am sure of this, that he who began a good work in you will bring it to completion at the day of Jesus Christ" (Phil 1.6).

Thankfully, the entire Trinity is involved in enabling us to remain faithful to the end. This should buttress our faith and bring us great comfort as we face trials and temptations along the way.

- God the Father — "My Father, who has given them to me, is greater than all, and no one is able to snatch them out of the Father's hand" (John 10.29).

- God the Son — "And this is the will of him who sent me, that I shall lose none of all those he has given me, but raise them up at the last day" (John 6.39 NIV).

- God the Holy Spirit — "And do not grieve the Holy Spirit of God, by whom you were sealed for the day of redemption" (Eph 4.30).[2]

---

[1] Eric J. Alexander, *Our Great God and Saviour* (Carlisle, PA: The Banner of Truth Trust, 2010), 112.

[2] This verse reminds us that the Holy Spirit is faithful to preserve us, but we also have a responsibility not to hinder or grieve him in this work.

Through Faith

In affirming God's power and faithfulness, it is important, however, not to overlook the prepositional phrase "through faith" in 1 Peter 1.5. God does not preserve us without our involvement. We must continue to believe in Jesus to endure to the end. So, how does God's power and our faith relate to each other in terms of preservation? Here are two wrong approaches. It is inaccurate to say that God's power keeps us whether we continue to have faith or not. Scripture says, "By faith you stand firm" (2 Cor 1.24 NIV). The idea of "once saved, always saved," in the sense that you can do whatever you want and even no longer believe and still be a Christian, is erroneous and dangerous. We must believe to be saved, and we must continue to believe to make it to heaven. There is no final salvation without perseverance in faith and obedience. It's not enough to begin the race; we must finish it to gain the prize (1 Cor 9.24-27).

Another inaccurate way of looking at the connection between God's power and our faith is to think that our faith causes God's power to keep us. This wrongly places the burden on us to endure. And the truth is that we would never endure if it primarily depended on us or our faith. The correct way to understand this verse is to realize that continued faith is essential for salvation but it is God's power that sustains our faith and strengthens it. A great example of this is when Peter denied Christ. Jesus said to him before his tragic denial, "Simon, Simon, Satan has asked to sift all of you as wheat. But I have prayed for you, Simon, that your faith may not fail. And when you have turned back, strengthen your brothers" (Luke 22.31-32 NIV). As was the case with Job, Satan was given permission by the Lord to attack the disciples. Satan attacked Peter in particular by tempting him to deny Christ, which he did three times (Luke 22.54-62). Jesus knew this in advance, so he not only warned Peter but assured him of his prayers.

This story reveals both our weakness and Jesus's power and faithfulness. Peter's weakness is highlighted in that Jesus refers to him as "Simon, Simon," not as Peter ("rock"). This is one of the rare places in Scripture where the Lord addresses someone by repeating their name, which shows the solemn nature of this statement.[3] Peter would deny Christ! An apostle would claim not to know who Jesus was! This was a serious lapse in his faith. If he could stumble like this, so can we if we're not prayerful and on guard (Matt 26.41; 1 Cor 10.12). But Peter's faith did not fail completely because Jesus had interceded for him. In the Greek the pronoun "I" is emphasized in the statement, "But *I* have prayed for you."[4] Jesus the Son of God is the one who prayed for Peter; therefore, his faith would not completely fail or cease to exist. It would be necessary for Peter to repent after this lapse, but notice it says "when you have turned back" not "if you turn back." Jesus's prayers were greater than Satan's attack. As with Peter, the intercession of Christ is key to our remaining faithful to Christ and not having a faith that gives out (Rom 8.34; Heb 7.25; 1 John 2.1-2). Jesus prayed for his disciples before he went to the cross, "I pray for them. I am not praying for the world, but for those you have given me, for they are yours...My prayer is not that you take them out of the world but that you protect them from the evil one" (John 17.9, 15 NIV). He is still praying this for us. Thank God we have Jesus at the right hand of God praying and interceding for us!

Therefore, we see that our faith is essential, but God is the one who strengthens and sustains our faith.[5] We must continue to believe to be saved, but the God who enabled us to believe initially can sustain our faith to the end. The same idea is emphasized near the conclusion of 1 Peter as well. In 5.8-11, it reads, "Be sober-minded; be watchful. Your adversary the devil prowls around like a roaring lion, seeking someone to devour. Resist him, firm in your faith, knowing that the same kinds of suffering are being experienced by

---

[3] There are seven people in Scripture addressed in this manner: Abraham (Gen 22.11), Jacob (Gen 46.2), Moses (Exod 3.4), Samuel (1 Sam 3.10), Martha (Luke 10.41), Simon Peter (Luke 22.31), and Saul of Tarsus (Acts 9.4; 22.7; 26.14).

[4] Robert H. Stein, *Luke* (Nashville: Broadman Press, 1992), 552.

[5] For other verses on how the Lord strengthens our faith, see Mark 9.24; Luke 17.5; Acts 14.22; 16.5; Rom 14.1, 4; Gal 5.5; Heb 12.2.

your brotherhood throughout the world. And after you have suffered a little while, the God of all grace, who has called you to his eternal glory in Christ, will himself restore, confirm, strengthen, and establish you. To him be the dominion forever and ever. Amen." We face trials and suffering, and we are the object of Satan's vicious attacks. Yet, the God of all grace himself is faithful to "restore, confirm, strengthen, and establish" us. He called us to his eternal glory and he will keep us until we arrive there. G. C. Berkouwer thus rightly notes, "Perseverance is a continuing miracle of His grace."[6]

Temporary Faith

Does this mean that it's impossible for a person to believe for a while then fall away? No, for Scripture teaches that there are those who fail to continue to believe. They have a temporary faith. We see this, for instance, in the Parable of the Sower. Luke 8.13 says, "And the ones on the rock are those who, when they hear the word, receive it with joy. But these have no root; they believe for a while, and in time of testing fall away." These people hear the gospel and believe, but their faith is shallow and it doesn't last. They are not necessarily hypocritical, but they simply make an emotional, impulsive response to the gospel and are never thoroughly rooted in the gospel. Thus, they are toppled when trials or persecution comes because of their faith. Here are a few other examples in the New Testament of faith that does not lead to final salvation because it is temporary, shallow, or merely intellectual, and thus because it is one or all of these things it is ultimately spurious, for it is not properly rooted in Christ nor does it endure.

- "Not everyone who says to me, 'Lord, Lord,' will enter the kingdom of heaven, but the one who does the will of my Father who is in heaven. On that day many will say to me, 'Lord, Lord, did we not prophesy in your name, and cast

---

[6] G. C. Berkouwer, *Faith and Perseverance* (Grand Rapids, MI: Eerdmans, 1958), 147.

out demons in your name, and do many mighty works in your name?' And then will I declare to them, 'I never knew you; depart from me, you workers of lawlessness'" (Matt 7.21-23). Some who confess Jesus as Lord and even perform miracles in his name will not enter the kingdom of heaven. Their faith was not genuine and obedient.

- "Now when he was in Jerusalem at the Passover Feast, many believed in his name when they saw the signs that he was doing. But Jesus on his part did not entrust himself to them, because he knew all people and needed no one to bear witness about man, for he himself knew what was in man" (John 2.23-25). Jesus did not trust some of those who believed in him, for he knew that their faith was shallow. They believed because of the miracles, not because they were truly devoted to him.

- "Even Simon himself believed, and after being baptized he continued with Philip. And seeing signs and great miracles performed, he was amazed. Now when the apostles at Jerusalem heard that Samaria had received the word of God, they sent to them Peter and John, who came down and prayed for them that they might receive the Holy Spirit, for he had not yet fallen on any of them, but they had only been baptized in the name of the Lord Jesus. Then they laid their hands on them and they received the Holy Spirit. Now when Simon saw that the Spirit was given through the laying on of the apostles' hands, he offered them money, saying, 'Give me this power also, so that anyone on whom I lay my hands may receive the Holy Spirit.' But Peter said to him, 'May your silver perish with you, because you thought you could obtain the gift of God with money! You have neither part nor lot in this matter, for your heart is not right before God. Repent, therefore, of this wickedness of yours, and pray to the Lord that, if possible, the intent of your heart may be forgiven you. For I see that you are in the gall of bitterness and in the bond of iniquity'" (Acts 8.13-23). Simon "believed" and was even baptized. But his faith was spurious, for he wanted to buy and distribute the power of the Holy Spirit for personal gain. His heart, according to Peter, was not right before God.

- "Among them are Hymenaeus and Philetus, who have swerved from the truth, saying that the resurrection has already happened. They are upsetting the faith of some. But God's firm foundation stands, bearing this seal: 'The Lord knows those who are his,' and, 'Let everyone who names the name of the Lord depart from iniquity'" (2 Tim 2.17-19). These two men had turned from the truth, but the Lord still knew who belonged to him. They are the ones who depart from iniquity and stay true to him.

- "What good is it, dear brothers and sisters, if you say you have faith but don't show it by your actions? Can that kind of faith save anyone?...So you see, faith by itself isn't enough. Unless it produces good deeds, it is dead and useless" (Jam 2.14, 17 NLT). It is not enough to simply believe in God's existence. True faith produces good deeds.

Unlike the faith mentioned above, saving, persevering faith is God-given and God-sustained. Paul speaks of "sincere faith" (1 Tim 1.5; 2 Tim 1.5). The word "sincere" has the idea of genuine, authentic, and unfeigned. Saving faith is sincere faith. It is more than an emotional response to the gospel. It understands the implications and cost of following Christ, and it endures knowing that great is our reward in heaven. Peter points out that not giving up when facing various trials proves the genuineness of one's faith, showing that it is real (1 Pet 1.6-7). Saving faith endures to the end. It is tried, it is weak at times, but it remains because God knows those who are his and he sustains them through every trial. "Through many dangers, toils and snares, I have already come; 'tis grace hath brought me safe thus far, and grace will lead me home."

The Perseverance of the Saints

At times people speak of eternal security or "once saved, always saved." The way many people understand this idea or the way they teach it is wrong. There is security in Christ, but it is not unrelated to how we live or believe. Others refer to the perseverance of the saints, which emphasizes the need for perseverance and makes it clear that this perseverance relates to saints, i.e., true believers. Another way of speaking of this is to call it the preservation of the saints, for it is God who preserves us. Either way, the emphasis is on the need and duty to remain true to the end. Here are some thoughts on the perseverance of the saints.

Only saints persevere. The only ones who persevere to the end are saints, and saints ("those set apart") are simply followers of Christ. If you are a Christian, then you are a saint. You are set apart by and for Christ at conversion. Only saints persevere. Once one of Wesley's preachers was asked by a Calvinist, "Do you believe in the perseverance of the saints?" He responded, "Certainly." The Calvinist was caught off guard and said, "I thought you did not." The Methodist preacher clarified, "O, Sir, you have been misinformed; it is the perseverance of *sinners* we doubt."[7] Only saints persevere and they must persevere as saints. If your faith is disingenuous or shallow then, you will not remain faithful to Christ when persecution or hardships come. That's why it's important to examine ourselves to see where we stand with the Lord (2 Cor 13.5; 2 Pet 1.10). Those who fall away were most likely never genuinely or thoroughly converted to begin with. They prayed a prayer or went to the altar or were baptized or shook the pastor's hand. But they did not truly repent of their sins and place their faith unreservedly in Jesus Christ.

---

[7] Iain H. Murray, *Wesley and Men Who Followed* (Carlisle, PA: The Banner of Truth Trust, 2003), 66.

Saints can persevere. God is willing and able to keep to the end those who belong to him. Jude 1.24-25 affirms, "Now to him who is able to keep you from stumbling and to present you blameless before the presence of his glory with great joy, to the only God, our Savior, through Jesus Christ our Lord, be glory, majesty, dominion, and authority, before all time and now and forever. Amen." He can preserve us through the fiercest trial or temptation. Thus, when apostasy occurs and unfortunately it does at times, it is not God's fault. It is ours. It shows that our faith was shallow and not properly rooted in the gospel. The warnings and conditional statements in Scripture show that we have a responsibility to persevere and not turn back (1 Cor 15.1-2; Heb 3.12-14). This should not upset or distress us, but it should lead to humility and ongoing dependence on Christ rather than on ourselves. Our hope is in Christ alone!

Saints must persevere. Jesus said, "The one who endures to the end will be saved" (Matt 24.13). There is no final salvation without perseverance. The idea that you can be eternally secure while living a lifestyle of unrepentant sin is simply unbiblical and dangerous. This teaching provides false assurance and can make people immune to conviction or conversion. We must properly balance the promise of God's preserving grace with the call for us to continue to believe and be faithful. In Jude, where we just looked at that beautiful doxology that speaks of God's ability to keep us, it also says, "Keep yourselves in the love of God" (v. 21). So, does God keep us or do we keep ourselves? Both are important. We are to watch and pray, seek the Lord, avoid temptation, and make use of the means of grace. But ultimately, it is God who preserves us by his power.

Saints will persevere.[8] Even weak saints will, according to Paul. In writing to the notoriously troubled church in Corinth, he

---

[8] There are those who believe for a while yet fall away from the gospel and are eternally lost (Luke 8.13). They fall away because their faith was shallow and defective. However, the elect—those whom God has chosen and thus knows will endure to the end—will never be lost. It is not possible for the elect to be led astray

refers to them as saints (1 Cor 1.2). He also speaks confidently of their endurance, which he roots in God's faithfulness rather than in their strength. He states, "He will also keep you firm to the end, so that you will be blameless on the day of our Lord Jesus Christ. God is faithful, who has called you into fellowship with his Son, Jesus Christ our Lord" (1 Cor 1.8-9 NIV). Interestingly, he says the Lord "will" keep them, not just that he can.[9] The same is true with Jesus's promise in John 10.28. However, this keeping by God is not mechanical or without the use of means. In this same letter, Paul warns of the danger of apostasy and urges them to persevere in faith in order to be saved in the end (1 Cor 9.24-27; 10.12; 15.1-2). Bruce Demarest notes, "The biblical representation of the believer's role in perseverance allows no room whatsoever for passivity, moral carelessness, easy-believism, or antinomianism. The Christian strives for godliness as if everything depended on him or her, while confident that the outcome ultimately rests with God."[10]

In light of this, I understand the doctrine of the perseverance of the saints to infer or teach the following.

- It does *not* mean that everyone who makes a profession of faith or is baptized will persevere to the end.

(Matt 24.24). By definition, the elect cannot become non-elect, for they were chosen before the foundation of the world. This is true even if one understands election to be based on foreseen faith. James Arminius himself made a distinction between non-persevering believers and elect believers who do persevere (Charles M. Cameron, "Arminius—Hero or Heretic?" *Evangelical Quarterly* 64.3 [1992]: 225-27). By the way, Augustine made a similar distinction (John Jefferson Davis, "The Perseverance of the Saints: A History of the Doctrine," *Journal of the Evangelical Theological Society* 34.2 [1991]: 213-14).

[9] Sam Storms shares five insights from 1 Corinthians 1.8-9. This is a promise not a wish, Christ is the one who sustains us, he sustains us to the end, he sustains us guiltless (via imputed righteousness), and we are assured of this because of God's faithfulness (*Kept for Jesus*, 90-92).

[10] Demarest, *The Cross and Salvation*, 450.

- It does *not* mean that you can live however you want and remain a Christian.

- It does *not* mean that true believers never stumble or even lapse in their faith for a while.

- It does *not* mean that God saves us or keeps us against our will.

- It does *not* mean that God preserves us in a mechanical, automatic fashion without the use of means including the warning of apostasy.

- It means that God is willing and able to preserve those who are truly saved through every trial and temptation.

- It means that "it is God who works in [us], both to will and to work for his good pleasure" (Phil 2.13), and thus we are able to work out our salvation with fear and trembling (v. 12).

- It means that saints are enabled to persevere in faith because God preserves them.[11]

---

[11] This is a notoriously difficult subject to address. The Bible promises that God will preserve us to the end while also warning against falling away. It's reassuring to me that even Luther and Arminius were not completely settled or unequivocal on this issue (Davis, "The Perseverance of the Saints," 215-16; Roger E. Olson, *Arminian Theology: Myths and Realities* [Downers Grove, IL: IVP Academic, 2006], 187). Wesley himself believed for a while that saints could not apostatize, at least those who were entirely sanctified couldn't. He later discarded this belief. However, he did believe that some could be given an assurance not only of their present salvation but of their perseverance to the end (Davis, "The Perseverance of the Saints," 223-24). Hopefully, we can agree that perseverance in faith is necessary to be saved and that God's love and power are greater than any temptation or trial we face in this life. As for me, I will trust in God to finish what he started in me. Therefore, with Paul I confidently affirm, "I know the one in whom I trust, and I am sure that he is able to guard what I have entrusted to him until the day of his return" (2 Tim 1.12 NLT). For a balanced, brief overview of the perseverance of the saints, see Robert E. Coleman, *The Heart of the Gospel* (Grand Rapids, MI: Baker Books, 2011), 197-210. For a few other works that attempt to take seriously both God's faithfulness and the warnings of

Salvation is by grace from beginning to end. I remember a preacher who once said that we are saved by grace but kept by works. I was a young Christian when I heard this statement, but I instinctively knew this was wrong. Grace saves us, sanctifies us, and preserves us. As Whitefield warned, "Build not on your own faithfulness, but on God's unchangeableness. Take heed of thinking you stand by the power of your own free will. The everlasting love of God the Father must be your only hope and consolation; let this support you under all trials."[12]

Saints persevere together. As mentioned earlier, the word "saint" is always plural in the New Testament. The only exception is Philippians 4.21, but the singular there is used in a collective sense ("every saint"). You can't be a saint in isolation and you can't persevere in isolation. We need the church. We need its prayers, encouragement, warnings, and accountability. To turn away from the church is to invite spiritual disaster. To be in Christ is to be in his body—the church. To remain in Christ is to remain in his body. Saints persevere together. That's why the church is so important and being involved in the fellowship of the church is not optional (Heb 10.24-25). Anyone who talks of the security of the believer but doesn't go to church or minimizes the importance of

---

apostasy, see Berkouwer, *Faith and Perseverance*; Thomas R. Schreiner, *Run to Win the Prize* (Wheaton, IL: Crossway, 2010); Charles G. Finney, *Lectures on Systemic Theology*, 2nd ed., ed. J. H. Fairchild (Whittier, CA: Colporter Kemp, 1946), 544-619; I. Howard Marshall, *Kept by the Power of God* (Minneapolis, MN: Bethany Fellowship, 1969). All of them view the warnings as real and needful, but Berkouwer, Schreiner, and Finney do not think true believers ever commit apostasy, while Marshall thinks it's possible but rare and unlikely. The emphasis in the New Testament certainly appears to be on God's faithful preservation of his saints, with this promised preservation being accompanied by the call and demand to persevere in faith to the end. The warnings are real and should shatter any spiritual apathy we have. Yet, the warnings should also drive us back to the promises, where we place our faith in God to keep us since we cannot do this on our own.

[12] Whitefield, "Christ the Believer's Wisdom, Righteousness, Sanctification, and Redemption" in *Select Sermons of George Whitefield*, 114.

church, that person is espousing ideas that are unscriptural. The church is our mother (Gal 4.26), and we need her help to endure to the end.

The Presence of God

I'd like to end this chapter and also this book with an emphasis on God's abiding presence with his people. This is a key, repeated motif in Scripture.[13] It is comforting to know the Lord is with us wherever we are and in the midst of whatever we're facing.

- "Have I not commanded you? Be strong and courageous. Do not be frightened, and do not be dismayed, for the LORD your God is with you wherever you go" (Josh 1.9).

- "So do not fear, for I am with you; do not be dismayed, for I am your God. I will strengthen you and help you; I will uphold you with my righteous right hand" (Isa 41.10 NIV).

- "Then Haggai, the messenger of the LORD, spoke to the people with the LORD'S message, 'I am with you, declares the LORD'" (Hag 1.13).

- "And behold, I am with you always, to the end of the age" (Matt 28.20).

- "And I will ask the Father, and he will give you another Helper, to be with you forever, even the Spirit of truth, whom the world cannot receive, because it neither sees him nor knows him. You know him, for he dwells with you and will be in you" (John 14.16-17).

- "Keep your lives free from the love of money and be content with what you have, because God has said, 'Never will I leave you; never will I forsake you'" (Heb 13.5 NIV).

---

[13] For a book that traces this theme throughout Scripture, see Lanier Burns, *The Nearness of God* (Phillipsburg, NJ: P & R Publishing, 2009).

Let me say a few words about this last verse, which states, "Never will I leave you; never will I forsake you." First, this is a *divine* promise. A promise from Scripture is a promise from God. It is made by God in the first person. It is most likely a quotation from Deuteronomy 31.6 or Joshua 1.5. God himself tells us he will never leave us. We can trust God's word. Second, it is a *personal* promise. The word "you" is singular. This is a promise to each and every child of God. That means it is a promise to you if you're saved. Third, it is a *guaranteed* promise. The word translated as "never" comes first in the Greek and occurs twice for emphasis. God will never leave his own not even for a millisecond. Fourth, this is a *practical* promise. The context is the call to contentment. How do we overcome greed and trust in God to provide for us? By knowing he is with us and will therefore take care of us. Last, it is a *sufficient* promise. If God himself is with us, what else do we need? He is enough, and he will be with us to the end.

God has saved us, and he will be faithful to us to the end. We enjoy his presence now, and we will enjoy his presence in the world to come. Then we will have full, immediate, ever-conscious access to his glorious presence for all eternity. "And I heard a loud voice from the throne saying, 'Behold, the dwelling place of God is with man. He will dwell with them, and they will be his people, and God himself will be with them as their God. He will wipe away every tear from their eyes, and death shall be no more, neither shall there be mourning, nor crying, nor pain anymore, for the former things have passed away'" (Rev 21.3-4).

BIBLIOGRAPHY

Alexander, Eric J. *Our Great God and Saviour*. Carlisle, PA: The Banner of Truth Trust, 2010.

Berkouwer, G. C. *Faith and Perseverance*. Grand Rapids, MI: Eerdmans, 1958.

Bolt, Peter G. *The Cross from a Distance*. Downers Grove, IL: InterVarsity, 2004.

Brown, Charles E. *The Meaning of Salvation*. Anderson, IN: Gospel Trumpet, 1950. Reprint, Salem, OH: Schmul Publishing, 1982.

Buchanan, James. *The Doctrine of Justification*. Carlisle, PA: The Banner of Truth Trust, 1997.

Bunyan, John. *Grace Abounding to the Chief of Sinners*. New York: Penguin Books, 1987.

Burns, Lanier. *The Nearness of God*. Phillipsburg, NJ: P & R Publishing, 2009.

Calvin, John. *The Institutes of Christian Religion*. Edited by Tony Lane and Hilary Osborne. Grand Rapids, MI: Baker Academic, 1987.

Cameron, Charles M. "Arminius—Hero or Heretic?" *Evangelical Quarterly* 64.3 (1992): 213-27.

Clowney, Edmund P. *The Church*. Downers Grove, IL: InterVarsity, 1995.

Davis, John Jefferson. "The Perseverance of the Saints: A History of the Doctrine." *Journal of the Evangelical Theological Society* 34.2 (1991): 213-28.

Demarest, Bruce. *The Cross and Salvation*. Wheaton, IL: Crossway Books, 1997.

Dunn, James D. G. *Baptism in the Holy Spirit*. Philadelphia: Westminster Press, 1970.

_____. *Romans 1-8*. Nashville: Thomas Nelson Publishers, 1988.

Erickson, Millard J. *The Concise Dictionary of Christian Theology*. Rev. ed. Wheaton, IL: Crossway Books, 2001.

Eveson, Philip. *The Great Exchange*. Bromley, England: Day One Publications, 1996.

Fee, Gordon D., and Douglas Stuart. *How to Read the Bible for All Its Worth*, 4th ed. Grand Rapids, MI: Zondervan, 2014.

Ferguson, Sinclair B. *The Holy Spirit*. Downers Grove, IL: InterVarsity, 1996.

Finney, Charles G. *Lectures on Systemic Theology*. 2nd ed. Edited by J. H. Fairchild. Whittier, CA: Colporter Kemp, 1946.

González, Justo L. *A Concise History of Christian Doctrine*. Nashville: Abingdon Press, 2005.

Green, Michael. *"But Don't All Religions Lead to God?"* Grand Rapids, MI: Baker Books, 2002.

_____. *The Meaning of Salvation*. Vancouver, BC: Regent College Publishing, 1998.

Harvey, John D. *Anointed with the Spirit and Power*. Phillipsburg, NJ: P & R Publishing, 2008.

Jeffery, Steve, Michael Ovey, and Andrew Sach. *Pierced for Our Transgressions*. Wheaton, IL: Crossway, 2007.

Jones, E. Stanley. *Christian Maturity*. Nashville: Abingdon Press, 1957.

Letham, Robert. *The Work of Christ*. Downers Grove, IL: InterVarsity, 1993.

Longmann III, Tremper. *Making Sense of the Old Testament*. Grand Rapids, MI: Baker Academic, 1998.

Macleod, Donald. *The Person of Christ*. Downers Grove, IL: InterVarsity, 1998.

Marshall, I. Howard. *Kept by the Power of God*. Minneapolis, MN: Bethany Fellowship, 1969.

McGrath, Alister E. *Theology: The Basics*. 2nd ed. Malden, MA: Blackwell Publishing, 2008.

Mohler, R. Albert. *Acts 1-12 For You*. Purcellville, VA: The Good Book Company, 2018.

Moo, Douglas. *The Epistle to the Romans*. Grand Rapids, MI: Eerdmans 1996.

Morris, Leon. *The Epistle to the Romans*. Grand Rapids, MI: Eerdmans, 1988.

Mounce, Robert H. *Romans*. Nashville: Broadman & Holman Publishers, 1995.

Murray, Iain H. *Wesley and Men Who Followed*. Carlisle, PA: The Banner of Truth Trust, 2003.

Olson, Roger E. *Arminian Theology: Myths and Realities*. Downers Grove, IL: IVP Academic, 2006.

Packer, J. I. *"Fundamentalism" and the Word of God*. Grand Rapids, MI: Eerdmans, 1958.

Piper, John. *Counted Righteous in Christ*. Wheaton, IL: Crossway, 2002.

Schreiner, Thomas R., and Shawn D. Wright. *Believer's Baptism*. Nashville: B & H Academic, 2006.

Schreiner, Thomas R. *Run to Win the Prize*. Wheaton, IL: Crossway, 2010.

Stafford, Gilbert W. *The Life of Salvation*. Anderson, IN: Warner Press, 1979.

Stein, Robert H. *Luke*. Nashville: Broadman Press, 1992.

Storms, Sam. *Kept for Jesus*. Wheaton, IL: Crossway, 2015.

Stott, John. *Baptism & Fullness*. Downers Grove, IL: InterVarsity, 1977.

_____. *The Message of 2 Timothy*. Downers Grove, IL: Inter-Varsity, 1973.

Thomas, Derek W. H. *How the Gospel Brings Us All the Way Home*. Orlando, FL: Reformation Trust, 2011.

Tomkins, Stephen. *John Wesley: A Biography*. Grand Rapids, MI: Eerdmans, 2003.

Tyerman, Luke. *The Life of the Rev. George Whitefield*. 2 vols. New York: Anson D. F. Randolph, 1877.

Vickers, Brian. *Justification by Grace through Faith*. Phillipsburg, NJ: P & R Publishing, 2013.

Watson, Thomas. *A Body of Divinity*. Carlisle, PA: The Banner of Truth Trust, 2003.

Wellum, Stephen. *Christ Alone: The Uniqueness of Jesus as Savior*. Grand Rapids, MI: Zondervan, 2017.

Wesley, John. *The Works of John Wesley*. 3rd ed. Peabody, MA: Hendrickson Publishers, 1991.

Whitefield, George. *Select Sermons of George Whitefield*. Carlisle, PA: The Banner of Truth Trust, 1990.

Witherington III, Ben. *The Living Word of God*. Waco, TX: Baylor University Press, 2009.

Wright, Christopher J. H. *Salvation Belongs to Our God*. Downers Grove, IL: IVP Academic, 2007.

CPSIA information can be obtained
at www.ICGtesting.com
Printed in the USA
FFHW020820141218
49879395-54471FF